DO YOU TEACH?
views on college teaching

Hugh Hildreth Skilling

Stanford University

Holt, Rinehart and Winston, Inc.

New York   Chicago   San Francisco   Atlanta   Dallas

Montreal   Toronto   London   Sydney

Foreword

For the prospective teacher

The purpose of this book is to help you as you teach; it is not intended to give you instructions, but perhaps it will offer guidance as you develop your own work in your own way. It is a narrative of a seminar for graduate students who plan to teach. From the first meeting at which Dr. Terman, vice-president and provost, tells of the criteria by which a university judges its applicants, to the discussion of learning by Dr. Hilgard, professor of psychology, the speakers at this seminar bring facts and theories, attitudes and insights, which the prospective teacher *wants* to know.

For the experienced teacher

Although teaching is an art—an art that must be developed by each teacher in the light of his own experience—may he not profit by considering the experience of others? The speakers at these seminars—Polya of mathematics, Vennard of engineering, Kirkpatrick of physics, and many others—have one thing in common: they were selected (by the students themselves) as outstandingly good teachers. In these chapters you will listen to the words of masters—*and, having listened, you can then adopt them, ignore them, or deny them as you see fit.*

For the professor who offers guidance

Departments for scientific subjects often offer guidance to prospective teachers, and departments of education and educational psychology always do so. *Could this book serve you by supplementing your own course on teaching methods or your own seminar for young teachers?* Should you bring this book to the attention of prospective teachers?

For the college and school administrator

Who is a good teacher? How do students learn? Should lectures, laboratories, or discussion groups be stressed? What of research? Why publish? How 'modern' can education be? What are other colleges thinking and doing? These questions are in many minds. *The accomplished men who speak in these chapters have something to say to you.*

H.H.S.
Stanford, California
March, 1969

Preface

Seminar leaders in these chapters are real people whom you may know.* The ideas expressed are their own and are published with their permission. The seminar class is a genuine class, and student members of the seminar, though individually fictional, are typical students and offer typical comments. The reader will, I am sure, recognize acquaintances among them.

H. H. Skilling

---

*Biographical information about the seminar leaders is given at the end of the book.

Seminar afternoons

Eleven Commandments for Teachers

The good teacher likes his students and enjoys helping them, understanding their thoughts and feelings. You should:

1. *Remember the students whom you teach, for they alone are the measure of your success.*
2. *Forget yourself, for your own excellence is good only as it helps your students.*
3. *Consider the purpose of your teaching, and show the student a goal as far ahead as you both can see.*
4. *Accept him as he is and improve him as you can; the student is guided by intellect but driven by emotion— to complain is futile, and to ignore his motivation is to fail.*
5. *Show him the real world of fact for interest and the ideal world of theory for understanding, each illuminating the other.*
6. *Relate new thoughts to what the student knows, for this is how he learns; lead him from the known to the unknown.*
7. *Repeat and repeat, yet never the same; let each idea be seen three times in different lights.*
8. *Let the student work, for work is remembered long after words are forgotten. Hearing is weak, seeing is better, doing is best.*
9. *Let the student seek; lead him to discoveries of his own, and these will be his choicest jewels of knowledge.*
10. *Provide light and air and quiet, for all your work is lost if attention fails.*
11. *Know thoroughly the subject that you teach, and where it leads; present it with interest and enthusiasm.*

1

From
the front office

"In answer to your question," said Dr. Terman to the young men in my seminar, "there are several things that a new teacher ought to do to establish himself."

I had introduced Dr. F. E. Terman to my seminar as a professor and head of electrical engineering, then dean of engineering, then provost and vice president of the university—as a man who showed genius in the choice of faculty members for his department, college, or university. I mentioned, of course, that he was even better known to the professional world as an author and a director of research, although these attainments would have less bearing, perhaps, on the day's discussion of young men on faculties.

"First you must develop real competence in some area of importance. Of course, you will be given classes to teach. Maybe you will have a chance to teach classes in subjects that you particularly like. But perhaps you won't.

"Anyway, pick a subject that you want to specialize in. Then you must learn all there is to know about that subject. Of course, it can't be a very broad subject at the beginning. Take an important subject that good men are interested in. Never mind if it is rather narrow, but go into it as deeply as possible. Read everything that has been written on that subject. Start with a subject that you know a good deal about already; this shouldn't be too hard if you have just been doing graduate study."

"Is it important what the subject is about?" asked Peter.

"Well, not so very much," replied Dr. Terman. "Naturally it has to be a subject in which a lot of good men around the country are interested. You don't want to be all by yourself with it. But apart from that it doesn't matter a great deal. New or old? No, that won't make much difference.

"Then find out what everybody else is doing. Get out among others who are important in the field. Go visiting and go to meetings. Ask questions. Everybody likes to talk about what he is doing. In this way you get to know the men who are working in your area, and they come to know you. This business of knowing them, and being known by them, is awfully important."

Dr. Terman was perhaps speaking from his background of science and engineering, but his points were not limited to any one discipline. As provost he had dealt with young teachers throughout the university.

"But how do you look for a subject for research?" asked Philip.

"Well, you don't really have to look for a subject. You soon find that you have read all there is, and that something you want to know about has never been published. You ask people who ought to know, and they don't have the answer. As far as you can tell there is just a gap in everybody's knowledge of the subject. All right; if it looks interesting and worthwhile, you start to find out about it. This is research."

"Do you mean that we should find out about it by experiment or by paper and pencil?" Philip inquired.

"Either one," Dr. Terman replied. "Experimental work in the laboratory is a sound and substantial kind of work, but theoretical investigation is all right in some areas, too.

"Then, when you have enough new material, you can write it up for publication. That is how your work gets to be known, and you begin to have a reputation in your professional subject.

"You must work to develop individuality, too. Write a book or something.

"And remember that your time is valuable. It's awfully easy to waste time. Be sure to teach well, but be careful about three things.

"First, it takes about as much time to teach a small class as a large one, and productivity is just as important to you as it is to the university where you work. You'll do a lot better to teach thirty or forty students than six or eight; besides, there's more satisfaction in it for you.

"Second, don't waste time on polishing up lecture notes to the last comma and semicolon. By the time you get the lectures just the way you want them, they'll be out of date.

"Third, don't fail to get new material into your courses every year. Your subject is changing all the time, and it is most important that you keep up with it. Research is one way to keep up to date. A man who is turning out good research has to know what's happening. Research is not the only way to keep up but it's a good way.

"Whatever you are doing, remember to keep up the productivity. With undergraduate students, don't limit your work to a handful of students. With PhD students, see that they get their thesis work done and their degrees granted and that they go on their way. With research, finish up jobs; don't let them hang on forever, but get a thing done, and publish a paper about it, and then go on to the next thing. There is no substitute for getting on with a job.

"I spoke a few minutes ago of the satisfaction that comes from having a class that is not too small," Dr. Terman reflected. "This touches on an important question: what *are* the satisfactions of a man in the teaching business? He probably isn't working primarily for money; if he is, he's made a mistake.

"For me the greatest satisfaction as a professor has come from working with individual people. Some of my students and boys I have worked with have gone on to be really important men. One is now near the top in government. Several are known all over the world in the electronics industry. One is a leader in research, and two are members of the National Academy of Science.

"As a dean, there is a satisfaction in getting good graduate programs going. There has been a great opportunity in recent years to get government research worked into graduate student programs, and this can help both the government and the students.

"As provost, guiding the university to excellence brings satisfaction. Building here, pruning there, keeping it all moving forward. . . . "

"Well," he paused, "Maybe you have some questions."

"Sir," said Peter, and he lost no time in pursuing this unexpected opportunity, "How do we go about getting our first job? Do we apply to one or several colleges, or do we wait for somebody to contact us?—or what?"

"It depends on a lot of things," said Dr. Terman. "In any case, for your first teaching position you really ought to get in touch with the heads of departments in several of the schools where you'd like to go. You can write to them or go to see them. Schools aren't all the same, but I can tell you what a school such as Stanford does.

"First, if we want a man with a reputation already established, a man to fill a top position, we start by building up a list of the best men in the country. We can begin this list with the names suggested by our own faculty, and add to it by asking a few outstanding men—senior statesmen in the profession—at other places. Then we attempt to determine the most promising names on our list, about three to six of them, and we get as much information on these as can be gathered without approaching them directly. Those that still look good are then approached, and frequently are invited to visit us. In the end we try to get the best available man to take the position.

"Quite often though, we are not looking for a man who already has a wide reputation. What we want is a young man with good promise but just starting. Then the best thing is to look for a young fellow just out of graduate school. To obtain a list of such young men we ask the professors in the top universities around the country who their best PhDs are. Those who look promising are investigated further. We read their papers, we visit them in their laboratories (but we don't say why), we call on them at their universities or in industry, and we ask their friends—and more particularly, their competitors—about them. In this way we find three or four whom we want to interview. Then we invite these men to come and see us, at our expense of course, and after that we are ready to make an offer.

"A university gains prestige by building steeples of eminence." Dr. Terman reverted to his view from the provost's office. "A uniform plateau of mediocrity does not make a great university. Steeples of excellence should be erected. Where a man is good, strengthen him. Where a department is notable, raise it. Put up the steeples in the mainstream. There is nothing harder to do than to keep your steeples in the mainstream, but nothing is more important.

"By and large, universities are not very efficient in using their resources, so there is a great opportunity for those that are. It came to be known around our provost's office as Terman's Law that 'The quality of a college program has little relation to the money spent on it.' Then there was Bowker's Corollary to this law (do you know Al Bowker?): 'Because much of the money is wasted anyway.' "

2
How to do it

The students did not leave when the hour was over. Most of them stood around in groups, talking to Dr. Terman or to me, asking questions and talking with each other. As often happened when the men of the seminar framed the discussion, it became personal and practical.

It was clear that Dr. Terman enjoyed talking with these young men who were soon to be teachers, but he had to catch an evening plane for New York, and after he left they asked questions of me.

"I am going to want a teaching job next year," said Peter. "It is now January. Should I write letters now, or when do I write letters? And what do I say?" Peter was nice looking, rather serious minded; he was now devoting most of his time to his dissertation.

"It is not too early to write letters now," I replied. "The best positions are probably being filled in the winter months. Of course, when there is any shortage of teachers there will be places available through the spring and even into the summer, but by that time the pickings are poor.

"The first thing that you personally have to consider is—where do you want to go? What are your restrictions or your preferences? Do you want a place on the East Coast or the West Coast? North or south? Big city or rural location? I've known men who wouldn't consider anywhere but New York City and others who thought Montana or Wyoming was about right. One wanted the tall, cool, forested mountains of the northwest. He went to Florida! But actually you often can have your preference.

"The next question is, what kind of a school do you want? Large or small? State or private? One with an established program or one just being built up? You can't always make this kind of choice just the way you would like to, but you might as well be prepared.

"And the level. Do you want a university that is largely graduate, an undergraduate college, a junior college, or what? Usually you know what you would like in this classification and which level would best match your ability and interest.

"Well, so much about the kind of school you want to work for. Now about the schools. There are all kinds, from the universities of highest prestige, which are pretty hard to get into, to colleges that were started last week and need a whole new faculty. From your point of view as prospective teachers, there are three kinds.

"First, there are universities at which you might like to work, but you never hear of their having vacancies. With these, you have to take all the initiative. You must be prepared for them to put up an impersonal and automatic resistance, because places that attract you may well attract others. What you need is a friend at court. Visit the university and talk with the professors in your line of work. If a faculty man at your own college has a personal friend at the school, get him to write to his friend about you—and the higher the professional standing of the writer, the better.

"Then go and talk with the professors and with the head of the department. Maybe talk with the dean. This is not to make your sales pitch but just to get acquainted. After this, write a letter to the head of the department, and if they expect to have an opening—and if you have made a good impression—you'll go on their list. Then you wait. But don't fail to apply to other places, too, for even if you rang the bell and they want you, there may be no vacancy for a while.

"The letter to the department head can be brief. One page of letter and a page of biographical information are enough. Give your schools, degrees, experience, and publications if any. Give the names and addresses of two or three references to whom they may write or phone about you—men who know you and your work and who are known in their profession. (It is courteous to ask permission of your references first, and besides it helps them to have you in mind when the time comes.)

"Then there are several dozen perfectly good universities, state universities and the like, that usually take the initiative to find a new man. A representative, sometimes the department head, may visit your university to ask about the young men who are expecting degrees within a few months and who might be interested in their kind of opening. If they don't come to you, a letter to them will get a quick response and probably an invitation to visit them at their expense.

"What kind of letter do you write to this kind of college? Oh, about the same as I spoke of just now: a page or two saying that you are interested and a page or two of biographical data. Don't send too much; it just clutters up the files.

"Then I think we can put in another class those colleges that have a lot of vacancies to fill quickly. Perhaps they are growing fast, or for some other reason they are badly in need of faculty. These schools often send out letters to most everybody everywhere. If they don't fill all their positions in the spring, they will still be hoping for candidates in August, so never give up. As in markets for all kinds of commodities, their specifications and requirements will get lower as September approaches. I cannot predict, though, that the salaries they offer are likely to go up, for salaries are usually fixed in some way or other.

"What kind of a degree do you need? Well, a doctorate is really almost necessary for a teaching job, except in junior colleges. There's a trend that way and you can't buck it. Even a little place like Camembert College that doesn't do any research, and doesn't expect to, may quite likely insist on a PhD or a DSc for a permanent faculty job.

"Why? Oh, I suppose a doctorate ensures several years of postgraduate study and suggests a good intelligence. But even more it is a status symbol: if a college takes a man with a mere master's degree, its academic neighbors say pooh-pooh. Only the obviously first-class colleges can have men without doctorates on their faculties. These universities can have professors with experience instead of degrees—and that is not going to make any difference to you in your first position. You will have to have a doctorate now or in prospect to get the kind of job that most of you want. This does not apply—at least not yet—to junior colleges.

"Yes, faculty men move around quite a lot from one college to another. Such a move is usually between colleges of a somewhat similar nature. It is unusual for a faculty man to move from a state university to Princeton or MIT or Harvard, or vice versa, but it does happen—both ways. On the other hand, there is a myth that if you are in a midwestern state university, the only way to get promoted is to move to another midwestern state university, but I expect this myth is now archaic. The great hunting grounds, according to this myth, were the meetings of professional societies, where all the midwestern deans attended for the hunting and all the young teachers displayed their best antlers.

"We scorn this myth, of course, but still it is probably good judgment to expect that the kind of university you start with is the kind in which you are likely to spend much of your life.

"Should you have a few years of experience in industry before you settle down to teaching? I think the answer depends on what you are planning to teach and where. If you will be teaching a pure science—such as physics, chemistry, biology, mathematics, or psychology—the advantage to you lies in starting your teaching work as soon as you have your doctorate.

"But suppose you are just about to receive a doctorate in an applied science and you have had no practical experience, then what? There is no question that you need some knowledge of what goes on in industry. How can you get this knowledge? Two or three years of full-time work in industry is one way. Industrial work in summers is another way, but this fills up the months that you would probably like to have free for research. Consulting work for industry that can be done in addition to your regular teaching job is still another way. A good many colleges will allow you a day a week for consulting work; however, there may not be any desirable consulting work to be done near your college.

"On the whole, you will have to play this one by ear. Just remember that your work will be pretty ineffective unless your teaching and research are soundly related to the real world.

"Do I mean to include all applied sciences teachers in this statement? Yes, I do. To some extent I include teachers of pure science and mathematics, too, if they are to teach students who will be the future engineers and chemists and geologists of the world. But, of course, it is the applied sciences people who find an acquaintance with industry most essential.

"Now I have been talking for a long time, and it all grew out of Peter's question about what you should do to get a teaching position. What else should I say?"

"Well, sir," asked Philip, "what do heads of departments want teachers to be like? What will they expect of us?" Philip hoped to teach some day, but he was still not far beyond his bachelor's degree in chemistry.

"That depends a lot on the man, of course, but I get a good many letters from heads of departments asking about applicants, and they all seem to have a good deal in common. They all ask, does he work well with others? Does he have originality, initiative, aptitude for research? What of his character, his personality? Also, unless the writer already has the man's academic record, the letter asks for his standing and whether he is among the top ten percent of our graduate students. This usually results, of course, in assurances that all our students are among the top ten percent.

"Of course, department heads always hope for faculty men with experience, and this you must tell them about. What jobs have you had? Have you done any teaching?

"It is particularly worthwhile to be able to tell them about teaching. Have you been a teacher already? Have you taught courses to undergraduates while you were a postgraduate student? Have you been in charge of a laboratory course? Here at Stanford, as you know, we have a sort of apprentice teaching arrangement where a graduate student can teach a course under guidance, and a chance at this is like gold in a gold mine. If, on some future registration day, you have a choice between taking a new course that you have never had or teaching, and there isn't time to do both—do the teaching. Taking a course is just adding to the dozens you have already taken, but teaching is a new experience. And you *learn* from teaching—golly, how you learn.

"Another thing—have you published any technical papers? Publications are excellent to talk about. Of course, when you are looking for your first teaching position it is not likely that you will have any, but later on when you want a place as associate professor or higher, the list of publications is almost decisive. The publications that really count are papers in a national journal for which the articles are selected (refereed, it is called) with a good deal of care. Or, of course, books. Having a paper published in a refereed journal means that your work has been considered and approved by an independent expert and this is great kudos."

"Should we send letters of recommendation when we write about a job?" asked Philip.

"Not until they are asked for, I think. Just give two or three good references, mutual acquaintances preferably and men who stand well in their fields.

"Remember that letters of recommendation have to be taken with grains of salt. Suppose Dr. Jones has been teaching for a year or two at Tillamook Tech, and I get a letter from his dean saying, 'We hear that Dr. Jones is applying to your university for a position. We are delighted, and we highly recommend this great step forward in Dr. Jones' career.' Do I hire Dr. Jones? Not on the strength of that letter I don't; it is an awful temptation to recommend a man for the sake of getting rid of him, and a glowing letter is likely to strain my confidence in the dean at Tillamook Tech unless he is a man I know and trust."

"Which requirements for a job do *you* think are the most important?" pursued Philip.

"Well, education is certainly one. Do you have a doctorate, and if so, where and when, with which professor, and in what subject? No doubt your education is highly specialized; do you have the breadth of mind to keep up with changes in your subject? Or to be a leader in an entirely new subject when the need comes? If I may take examples of what I mean from electrical engineering, think of vacuum-tube men who jumped into solid state, or electromagnetic men who found a new joy in lasers, or linear-network men who now delight in the nonlinear.

"Have you shown an ability to get things done? Do you look for jobs and then finish them up? Are you a good man to work with—friendly and helpful, not antagonistic nor too selfish? And above all, will you be a good teacher?"

"How can anybody tell if a man will be a good teacher?" wondered Peter.

"This is surely the big question," I admitted. "There are several ways of finding a partial answer, but getting a really satisfactory assurance of good teaching is not easy.

"I have often wondered whether there is any way to get an idea of teaching ability quickly. I sometimes ask myself, 'What is there about a man that makes him a good teacher?' I know that a man is often believed to be a good teacher because he is known to have given a good talk to a departmental colloquium or because he has done well in presenting a paper to a professional organization, but this is surely not the whole story. Necessary but not sufficient? Yes, that just about describes it.

"I think that if I had to decide on the basis of one criterion alone (which the Lord forbid), it might well be this: *Does he like students? Does he like teaching? Does he really want to explain things, even to a student who is a little stupid? And, above all, can he understand how?*"

"You mean, does he understand the subject well enough to explain it?" asked James.

"Oh, no; any fairly bright man can understand the subject. I mean, can he understand the student, why the student is having trouble, where the student has gone wrong, and what words to use to help this particular student? This is really a rare ability—perhaps it is the art of the teacher."

3

The profession of professing

"If you can grasp the essentials and pass them on to other people in such a way that they can grasp the essentials more easily than you did, then you're a teacher." Professor Linvill proposed this simple test to the young men of the seminar. John Linvill was professor of electrical engineering and head of the Stanford department. His personal interest was in solid-state circuits, but in introducing him I had dwelt on his broad view of science and engineering. His delightful personality I knew would be apparent.

"Our teaching in college is mostly just patterned on our own experience of learning. We tend to copy the teachers who did a pretty good job on us, with some improvements of our own added.

"The usual stereotype of a teacher is a lecturer, and of course lecturing is, and probably always will be, central to teaching; but there are a good many different combinations of learning processes that are part of the educational operation. I'll just list some of them here on the blackboard, and I will put them in ascending order of student participation. We can call this the *Environment of Education*, and begin with *reading*. Here a student reads books, which might be the textbook in the course; and notes, perhaps including his own; and current periodicals or other references. There is obviously no opportunity for the student to *do* anything about it, unless he might do some problems in a textbook; he just reads.

"The second category is *lectures*. Lectures have several purposes. They will establish the structure of the subject, and they can do this better than a book because the range of emphasis in lectures is greater than that possible in books. Also they will guide the attention of the student and give an opportunity to illustrate techniques. Another thing, lectures provide an opportunity for interactive communication between student and teacher, a kind of verbal feedback, which can be extraordinarily helpful because it can influence what the teacher says to the class as he goes along.

"Third in the order of student participation is *individual directed study*. I want to include in this category the work that the students do that is more than just reading or listening, such as home problems, quizzes, and the like, where the students actually do something themselves. This is often a problem-solving kind of job, a sort of do-it-yourself lecture, and it can be somewhat extrapolative and creative.

"Fourth, there is *individual undirected study*, and this is just about the same thing as *research*. The difference between this and directed study is that here you make up the problem yourself and then go ahead and solve it. A student has to find a new solution to a new problem, and it is an explorative and vague kind of business. It is the maximum of extrapolation and creativity, and we teachers can't do much but give encouragement to a student after we have him started in a hopeful direction. You just talk with the student about this and that and about the kind of work that might be worth doing, and pretty soon you see his ears light up.

"In a university environment there are always other students and faculty people around who are doing similar things in research, and there is a chance for interaction with them. This is really pretty important. If a man had to do his job all by himself he'd be kind of lonesome: and besides he wouldn't have anybody to show his results to so they could criticize and help him, and he could help them, and he could know what else was going on and what other people were thinking about. This kind of personal contact is a good part of the university environment.

"A rather special thing about the teaching process is that our output is *people*, not autos or TV sets or bridges. The success of us teachers is measured by the changes we make in people. This is a very difficult commodity to measure, and in fact we don't really know just how. Teaching is more complicated than maximizing the design of a girder or computing the current in a circuit.

"What we teach changes a little every year, or at least it sometimes changes a little and sometimes it changes quite a lot. This is one of the pitfalls of the teaching business; the commodity we sell doesn't ever stand still, you know. Teaching is different from the grocery business or paving or painting or truck driving because a teacher has a vested interest in change. This is really a unique sort of a situation, and it's very attractive to the kind of men who belong in college teaching.

"If you are doing elementary teaching, an awful lot depends on how you do it and on what are called 'teaching techniques.' Of course, the way you teach continues to be important all the way up into graduate school, but by the time you get to graduate school there has to be a good deal more emphasis on course content, too.

"The objective all along is for the student to acquire knowledge, but by the time he is doing graduate work he is getting ready to go out on his own and do something beyond what he has learned in class, and then you also have to promote his extrapolative ability, or his creativeness if you want to call it that.

"Some objective, such as acquiring knowledge and then learning to use it and to extrapolate a little bit has to be the goal of a teacher and of the men in his class, I expect, and there must be a little conformity with some such sort of goal or there will be complete chaos, and that would be pretty bad. Yet perhaps there must always be a little chaos. Some teachers are very orderly but a little bit lacking in imaginative characteristics, and on the other hand you might be able to think of some other teacher who would be very imaginative but who ran in such a hit-or-miss way that he just couldn't be counted on at all. We can probably get along with a few of these, of each kind. But if you find a teacher who says he doesn't like people, then he's probably in the wrong business.

"A year or two ago, you may remember, there was a second-hand car salesman down here on the highway who called himself 'The Count of El Camino' and who 'loved cars but hated money'. Well, maybe this has some suggestion for a teacher.

"Then practically all teachers have to do some of the administrative work within the university and this usually means committee work, because there are a lot of committees in a university. A university is an unusual operation, and the best industrial managers would probably not choose a university environment in which to manage. A university tends to be a community of independent scholars, and they like this independence, so administration is quite different from what it is in other organizations. Quite a good deal is done through committees, and these bring you into contact with other professors in adjacent interests and can be pretty worthwhile.

"Another facet of being a professor is writing. Lecturing leads to writing as your class notes become books; research leads to writing of a different kind—publication in professional journals and research monographs. All this is a pretty good thing to do, because a lot of people will get to know you through the things you write.

"The publicity of publication is good for you personally because it can mean that hundreds or thousands of the people who count in your field will find out who you are and that you really know what you are talking about. Other people who are doing the same kind of work will want to know what you are doing, and they will tell you what they are doing, too. Publication is the way into a sort of professional community.

"Publication is good for your university, too, for it makes the university known as a place where good work is done. Your department head and your dean will be glad when you publish, and you may even find this reflected in your salary or your promotion. At least, a faculty man who doesn't publish can count on being given more routine jobs than a faculty man who does publish.

"Industrial contact is another good part of a university environment. It is good for faculty people as well as students to have some contact with industry and to know what is going on. Any engineer's job is to solve someone else's problems, and if a professor does a little consulting for industrial companies, he can find it both interesting and profitable, and if it is done right, it can make him a better professor.

"There can be a point of view in industry that is different from what you might find in the university, too. When I went from MIT to Bell Labs I found that I had overlearned a narrow area. I needed to know about more subjects than just network theory, and there were some small matters on which I had more knowledge than there was any real use for. Nobody can know everything about everything, but MIT had tended to give me too much about too little.

"One characteristic of a good industrial research man that probably makes him different from a good teacher is that he often has to come up with the right answer without sufficient evidence. There is a limit to what is known about something and a limit to the time that he can spend exploring all the possibilities, but still he must not make any considerable mistake. There is a very heavy responsibility on an engineer in industry to get an answer quickly and to get it right.

"Another part of a teacher's time goes into professional society activities. These are sometimes very worthwhile for the contacts with people and the knowledge of matters that are important. Another closely related activity is a role in government, where a professor can sometimes act as an independent expert without an axe to grind. This kind of thing is all very useful no doubt, and good to a certain extent, but universities naturally view such involvement with some misgivings when it begins to reduce a faculty man's time with his students.

"I really suppose that quite a lot of what I have said applies primarily to American universities," concluded Professor Linvill. "I spent a year not long ago at the Swiss Institute of Technology, and the students there are a good deal more freewheeling than ours. They don't seem to take so much supervision. But by and large, a university one place is pretty much like a university somewhere else."

Professor Linvill smiled at me, and I turned to the seminar for questions and discussion. Andrew remarked happily, "I sure learned a lot about getting out an answer in a hurry when I was at Edam Electronics."

But Peter looked troubled. "You spoke about the change that is always going on in science and engineering," he said. "Doesn't this mean that what a teacher teaches is going to be obsolete very soon?"

"Yes," Professor Linvill replied. "It surely does. Anybody who is going to keep up with the things that go on in science the way it is moving these days is likely to have about three careers in his active lifetime, say something like twelve to fifteen years apiece. A man who knew quite a lot about vacuum tubes in 1940 had to learn a good deal about transistors in 1950 and some more about integrated circuits in 1960, and that man had it easy because those are not entirely different subjects. Think of the medical man who had to learn about vitamins in 1930 and then had to use antibiotics all of a sudden about 1945; or the aircraft man who had to cope with jet engines and then a few years later with supersonic aircraft.

"I suppose that a teacher's responsibility is to start a young man on his first career, and after that each man has to be his own teacher. Maybe if he can't do that for himself he can get some help from what is called *continuing education*. Of course books help out with learning new things when and as you need them.

"But a teacher ought to say to himself every time he starts to teach a new subject, 'Do I know that this is still going to be good stuff in another twenty or thirty or forty years?' If he can say 'Yes' as he can with calculus or mechanics or circuit theory, good; but if he has to say 'No, I don't really know whether it is or not', then he ought to be very sure that there is some other good strong justification for taking up the students' time.

"Maybe the material that the teacher is about to give is what a student will need in his first job, such as the characteristics of typical commercial transistors, and sometimes that's a pretty good reason for giving him some fairly specific stuff.

"Or maybe it is some theory that seems pretty remote from present reality but that might help a student open up a second or third career sometime in the future. Of course this is awfully hard to know, but it is really a good thing to do, because it is not very often that a man will open up an entirely new subject for himself after he has been away from school for a good many years. Even if he knows that he ought to start in and learn a new subject, he probably won't do it unless his school work has given him some kind of a foundation to build on.

"So this is a job for you teachers, and it's one of the toughest jobs you'll have to do—teach men now what they are going to need twenty or twenty-five or thirty years from now."

"Oh," moaned Thomas, but James's ears lit up.

4

Teaching is an art

My teaching seminar came drifting into the room on the next Thursday afternoon and found seats around the long table.

"At our first meeting," I reminded them, "I promised to ask some of our notably good teachers to come and talk with us. You gave me the names of some whom you wanted to hear, and I am happy to say that Professor Vennard agreed to come today.

"For the record, Professor J. K. Vennard is professor of fluid mechanics. He is internationally known as the author of *Elementary Fluid Mechanics*, which is one of the most widely used college texts on the subject and is now in, I believe, its fourth edition.

"However, in this seminar we are more interested in the fact that Professor Vennard is known to our undergraduates as one of the best teachers, one of the best advisers, and one of the most helpful men on our faculty.

"I haven't asked Professor Vennard for the subject of his discussion today; I just asked him to talk about what the young teacher ought to know, and he'll tell you the rest himself. Professor Vennard."

"Actually," said Professor Vennard, "I want to start with a few words about the guidance that a young teacher will get—or will not get—as he starts his first job in a university. Usually, as a matter of fact, he will get little or none. Older faculty members are either not interested or don't have the time. There is little staff discussion of teaching in general or of courses in particular.

"Does this mean that there is no real faith in the value of planning?

Apparently it does. As a result the progress of a new teacher is mostly by trial and error. Possibly this 'hands off' policy is better than a rigid guidance that stifles initiative, but it does seem that there ought to be some better middle ground.

"However, you will usually be on your own. An excellent job of teaching will bring compliments and even promotion, or a very poor job may lead to criticism from your superiors; but between these extremes you'll have to find your own way, set your own standards, and meet your own challenges. Your conscience is your guide." Professor Vennard paused to distribute some papers.

"Wouldn't it be nice if there were someone to help out new teachers?" suggested James brightly. "There could be somebody on each faculty and a seminar like this one, too."

"There isn't, though." John considered it a mission in life to subdue his ebullient brother.

"Sir," asked Philip, the young chemist, "does this mean that teaching is a poor way to spend your life?"

"Oh, no," replied Professor Vennard. "*It's not Utopia, but it's very pleasant.*

"What are the teacher's motivations and rewards? We hear quite a lot about the student's motivations; maybe somebody ought to think a little more about the teacher's motivations, too.

"Service to others, respect from others, authority over others, financial gain, security, opportunity for research—these are some of the motives, and people who are not teachers might add easy work and long vacations. The teacher himself knows that his work is not measured in hours and must always be done to do honor to a high profession.

"Rewards are mainly in the satisfaction of a good job done, a real service rendered, the success of students, and the respect of our students and our colleagues. Can we ask for more?

"*What the teacher is speaks a thousand times more loudly than what he says,*" quoted Professor Vennard. "Things that count are a teacher's *character* and his *attitudes*. According to Dean Potter, the good teacher is enthusiastic, kind, agreeable, accommodating, cooperative, patient, optimistic, inspiring, tactful, clear-thinking, courteous, sympathetic; he knows his subject and is willing to accept responsibility. Conversely, the poor teacher is sarcastic, conceited, snobbish, selfish, profane, intolerant, sloppy, unenthusiastic, and indifferent."

"Think of that," sighed Philip, under his breath. "Did you say 'angel'?"

"A comprehensive check list? Well, yes, it is. But character and attitudes can't be concealed from the student, so they had better be good. They may well be more significant than the subject matter, particularly in building character.

"Things like work habits, ethics, professional attitudes, courage, mental honesty, and punctuality are taught unintentionally by your example. The little things count heavily here and should be watched carefully.

"Setting a good example seems to be one sure way of inspiring the student whose main interest may be elsewhere. Does inspiration stem from stimulation of curiosity accompanied by just the right challenge? What is inspiration? How can you measure inspiration anyway?"

"Do we have to be all that to be teachers?" Philip tried to sound discouraged, but he was straight and alert.

"No, only to be *good* teachers."

"I thought all we had to do was buy a little book for fifteen cents on How To Be a Teacher," Philip mourned.

"Save the fifteen cents," urged Professor Vennard. "Teaching is an art, and an art cannot be mastered by reading about methods, however scientific the methods may be. Perhaps there are twenty different teaching methods, as some say, but you cannot swim by reading about strokes nor paint by learning to mix colors.

"Do learn the methods, though, and exploit the ones that appeal most to you and fit your personality best. Then you may hope someday to become a teacher."

"Teaching is an art?" murmured Peter.

"Teaching is an art," said Professor Vennard.

* * *

A five-minute intermission had been spent around the coffee machine for the February day was cool, and as the seminar men returned to their seats, Professor Vennard turned to the next page of his outline.

"*The Student*," he read, and looked up. "*He's no genius but is still well worth our best efforts.* In particular, *your* students. Overcoming limitations and distractions and putting youthful energy and enthusiasm to good use are the teacher's big challenge. Educational institutions are supposed to do many things, but we should hold to the naïve idea that their main job is to teach students."

"Oh, I say." James was startled. "Do you really . . . do you . . . I mean do you? . . ."

"Yes, I really do. There are universities. There are research organizations. There are institutes for advanced study. These may overlap, but they are not the same thing.

"Now why is your student in college? Perhaps to increase his earning power, to bolster his prestige, to fit the white collar social pattern, probably because his parents sent him. Maybe he likes college life and the extracurricular activities. Certainly not for study alone. He is not usually a scholar thirsting for knowledge for knowledge's sake. Realize this and make allowances.

"His capacities are all determined by factors beyond your control. Heredity, memory, intelligence—you can do nothing. Work habits—you cannot do much. Just remember that your students will always be the best that the admissions office can provide.

"Remember, too, that students are human and that they will react favorably to encouragement. A student usually requires encouragement to guide him through the curriculum. Since no two students are alike, the ideal would be to deal with him individually, but this is obviously impossible and a suitable compromise is the main problem. Teaching, as I said, is an art.

"How can his capacities be fully developed? Constant patience and encouragement in shooting for attainable goals—this is what the teacher can give, forcing responsibility upon him, forcing him to think and work diligently.

"How does he learn? First, you must stress fundamentals. Teach the rules, without all the exceptions. Second, try to apply principles repetitiously to different examples until the whole picture fits together. Only in Utopia is a student able to progress by deduction from the general to the specific."

"In where?" asked James; he had been taking notes.

"In Utopia," said Professor Vennard.

"Oh," said James.

"Then absorption time is necessary. If new ideas come too fast they just don't soak in. Probably this is the main obstacle to learning. Absorption time is very different for different students—some are quick, some are slow. This is not quite the same thing as intelligence. It is the time required for a man to relate a new idea to what he already knows. Older students, say over thirty, take more absorption time. Perhaps it is because they already know more—we hope so. Distractions take up the absorption time. That is why you must prevent distractions."

"Such as a pretty girl going by the window?" asked John wistfully.

"Well, that isn't exactly what I was thinking of," replied Professor Vennard, "but it will do. My own idea was something like hammering or pounding."

"Not so good," said John.

"Now," Professor Vennard turned another page, "we have talked a little about the teacher and a little about his students. Let's say something about his classroom. *The classroom is analogous to the studio of the artist or composer.*

"Student respect is not automatic; quite the contrary. It must be won in every class. It can be won only by mastery of the subject, good presentation, and goodwill toward the students. The students must have confidence in you.

"First impressions are likely to be lasting impressions, so watch the first class meeting. Students will follow the master teacher whether they love him or not, but it seems better human relations if an atmosphere of good feeling can be promoted. You don't have to be popular but it helps.

"Students respect the specialist but respect the widely educated specialist more. Know your field but strive to broaden your general education.

"Let the student feel that he is a vital part of the educational process. Somehow he must participate. He must think along with you in lecture classes and take part actively in recitations. He learns by doing more than by abstract thinking, and this is the value of good problems.

"Never forget rewards and punishments, compliments and admonitions. Never miss a chance to encourage and compliment originality.

"Recitation promotes student responsibility and participation. However, does any of us really believe that a well prepared lecture, replete with examples and analogies and presented with some showmanship, is useless in stimulating thought?"

"Did you say 'showmanship'?" asked Philip, doubtfully.

"I did indeed. Don't we all like a good show? Doesn't it make a better and deeper impression?"

"I sure like a good show," said John.

"I expect we all do," commented Professor Vennard. "Be enthusiastic no matter how many times you have presented the subject before. Remember that it's new to the student and can be stimulating if you make it so. The teacher can save himself from the boredom that sets in from repeated teaching of the same elementary material by his interest in how the material is received by each student.

"Objectives must be clear to both the teacher and the students. They should always be stated explicitly. Are you teaching facts or principles or methods? Be sure the students know. Is the subject matter really significant today? Does it have future use?

"The problems of graduate and undergraduate teaching are very different, and it is quite possible to be good at one and poor at the other. A young teacher usually begins with undergraduate teaching and aspires to graduate teaching. Be patient; you need more experience for graduate teaching."

"But sir," interposed James, "it seems to me it ought to be just the other way. Don't new PhD's know the graduate subject matter better, and can't more experienced teachers get better results with undergraduate classes?"

"Well, that seems to be a good point," replied Professor Vennard. "Maybe there is something to be said for starting new teachers on graduate classes. However, the fact of the matter is that the other way around is more usual. I think you'd better expect to teach undergraduates at first."

"How large will our classes be?" Philip inquired.

"That is going to depend on a lot of things. The ideal seems to be around twenty, but in practice, class size is dictated by space and economic factors beyond your control. Your obligation is to use the most effective method of teaching for the class you are given."

"I think," said James, idealistic as ever, "that it is not right to compromise with good teaching."

"Don't be a nincompoop," hissed John.

"Surely one must keep up his academic standards."

John refused the bait. "You can do what you want with your academic standards. Mine will be comfortably low."

Professor Vennard chose to ignore the byplay of the brothers. "Academic standards, I expect, will vary with the business cycle if the school is to remain solvent. Your job is to do your best with the students on the premises: obviously you can't do anything for those who might be there but aren't.

"Always remember that the end product is an educated man, not a lecture or a curriculum. These are means to the end.

"With that I shall stop and ask for questions."

Questions came quickly. "What about a textbook?" asked Peter.

"I think a good textbook is essential in an undergraduate course, though for a graduate course you might not always be able to find what you want.

The book must be carefully selected to fit the teacher and the course and the students. It ought to be written at the students' level, and they should be expected to get something from it before coming to class."

"Some teachers just say in class what is written in the book," complained Philip.

"Yes, that must be avoided or at least minimized. Some repetition is useful, but be careful, and use it with variety."

Peter asked, "What about examinations?"

"Well, the question is, do we measure knowledge or understanding? Personally I like examinations that require the application of principles to new situations, as in home problems. But in any case, grade exam papers carefully, indicate errors, return them promptly, and discuss them in class.

"Finally, I should like to add a personal observation. Treat students in the classroom as you would guests in your home. Discourtesy to a single student has a disastrous effect on the whole class."

5
Why a teacher?

"Sheer waste of time," said John, gazing at the ceiling.

"It is not!" James was indignant. "The teacher *is* important."

"Oh, just to pick up the homework papers. That's what you'll do when you're a teacher."

"Well, that isn't *all* I'll do. I'll . . . I'll. . . ."

"You'll do what?" John inquired of a spot on the ceiling. "What will you do that a machine couldn't do?"

Peter grinned as I came across the room. "It's just James and John again, sir," he explained. "James *does* rise so nicely when he's teased."

"I see. It's about teaching?" I asked.

"Oh, yes. John says a teacher doesn't really do anything much, and James gets all excited."

John had withdrawn his gaze from the ceiling, and seeing me he subsided into his notebook. James was still spluttering.

"Well, James," I asked, "What *will* you do when you are a teacher?"

But James was a little incoherent. "I want to show them how . . . I want to lead them into something new. . . ."

James found expression difficult, so I turned to the others of the seminar with the same leading question. "What *does* the teacher do?"

"Why, the teacher gives the lecture," said Philip.

"Must there be a lecture? Can't the students learn the subject just as well by reading the book, supposing it's a good book?"

"Well, the teacher has to answer his students' questions," suggested Peter.

"Would you have a teacher spend his whole hour in front of a class answering questions?"

"I don't suppose so," Peter agreed. "Maybe he can add things that aren't in the book and give examples from his own experience."

"About reading the book," said Andrew, "we did a lot of reading when I was working for Edam Electronics. We read a lot of books. But it wasn't the same as class work somehow. I don't know just what the teacher does, sir, but his being there sure makes a difference."

"But why?" I asked. "In fact, why should there be a teacher at all? Or even a university? Why can't a bright young man just get a dozen books and read them, and work the problems, and spend the same amount of time learning things that he might otherwise spend in college? Wouldn't that be just as good?"

"No," said Andrew, "he wants a degree to get a job."

"No," said Philip, "he wouldn't stick to it."

"No," said Peter, "there wouldn't be anybody to ask questions of."

"No," said John, "he wouldn't get his papers corrected."

"Do you really think," I urged, "that a university is as mechanical as all that? Is it just to grant degrees? Or to drive a boy to work when he doesn't want to? Or to correct homework papers? Why, a correspondence school will correct papers for you and even give a degree. Does that make it the same thing?"

"But, sir," urged James, "isn't there really some inspiration or something that the teacher gives? I mean, can't he make the class *want* to work? It seems to me that with some teachers I've really felt that learning was a good thing to do and I wanted to do it." James was earnest, but perhaps his words were inadequate; it seemed that he had never before explored in this direction.

"Some of the Education people talk about *rapport* or *empathy*," I suggested.

"Oh," said James. "Well, if a teacher can do what I mean, it's really important."

"Yes," I agreed, "It is. However, I sometimes wonder just where the dividing line comes between having a teacher and not having a teacher. Let me ask you a hypothetical question, and then you can tell me what you think of it.

"Suppose some university had a really good teacher on its faculty, and he was going to retire pretty soon. He was a splendid lecturer, and everybody liked him because of his fine personality. Students liked to be in his classes, but this made the classes large—too large for questions to be asked easily. Our university had just such a man in Stephen Timoshenko, whom many of you may know. He sometimes taught large classes in beginning mechanics.

"Now this is the question. Suppose the university had made a record of each of Professor Timoshenko's lectures exactly as he gave them. Suppose a movie had been taken, in color, showing Timoshenko lecturing and showing everything he wrote on the board, with the sound track recording everything he said so that no detail of the lecture was lost. Assume all this to be possible.

"Then, another year, when Professor Timoshenko had retired and gone to Europe, could this movie be played back to another class, and would it be just as good for the class to see the movie as to listen to Professor Timoshenko in person? What about it?"

My seminar took some time to consider this proposition. For a while there was no answer at all. Then Philip spoke.

"I don't think it would be the same, but I don't know why."

"It seems to me it would be all right," said John. "What's the difference?"

"I had a good job last year," said Andrew, "and I sure wouldn't have given it up and come back to college just to see a movie."

"Why not?"

"Well, for one thing, suppose I want to talk to the teacher. You can't talk back to a loudspeaker."

"Oh," I explained, "there would be a teaching assistant or an instructor who would meet with the class right after the movie for discussion. He could answer questions or explain anything that needed explaining. The movie would just give the lecture."

"Would you see the speaker on the screen, and do you see what he puts on the blackboard," asked Peter, "and do you hear what he says?"

"Yes."

"Well, isn't that about the same as television? Educational television?"

"Yes, and we shall suppose, for purposes of discussion, that this picture is in every technical way as good as television, with a larger, clearer picture and higher fidelity sound. We shall so assume."

"Then this movie ought to work, because television does."

"Yes, Peter, I think we can agree that it would surely work. But would it work as well as—the same as—having Professor Timoshenko in the room?"

"No," said Peter.

"Why not?"

"I don't know," said Peter, "but I've seen television."

"It sounds to me like a way for the university to save money at the expense of the students," complained Matthew, a small dark man whose skepticism was sometimes a little depressing.

"That," I objected, "is not the question. The question is, would it be as good? Yes, James?"

"Well, sir, I don't know just how to say it, but I think a student wants something more than a movie. He wants a teacher who will pay some attention to *him*, and . . . well, I mean, it's different somehow."

"Yes," I encouraged, "what's different?"

"Oh, the film is not really anything but a film, and a television tube is just a tube. There isn't any—well, any warmth. Nobody cares what a picture on a screen thinks."

"Does the student care what the teacher thinks when there is a real teacher giving the lecture?"

"Yes," said James, and there was a general nodding of heads.

"They do if they have any respect for the teacher," agreed Philip.

"Yes. That is about what I was trying to say. Besides," added James, "maybe a professor would help me out if I had problems or . . . or personal troubles. It seems to me that a fellow's whole life is worth something, as well as his technical learning, isn't it?"

"Yes," I said.

"Has a movie like this ever been tried?" asked Andrew, always practical.

"Well," I temporized, "It has in a way. But first let me tell you about a time several years ago when Professor Kirkpatrick of our physics department had to be away in the middle of the term. Professor Kirkpatrick was to be awarded the Oersted medal of the American Association of Physics Teachers for excellent teaching. It was to be at a meeting in New York and he wanted to go, but at the same time he wanted to take care of the class that he was teaching here that term. The class was in elementary physics, a large class of over a hundred in a big lecture room. What Professor Kirkpatrick did was to put his lectures on tape and have the tape played back to the class while he was in New York.

"Before Professor Kirkpatrick left he gave his lectures, but only to a tape recorder and a technician. The technician was the man who set up the apparatus for Professor Kirkpatrick's demonstrations. I ought to say that Professor Kirkpatrick gives excellent demonstrations and that the technician was unusually capable.

"Well, Professor Kirkpatrick asked me to visit his class on one of the days that he was away to see how the taped lecture went. I can say at once that it went very well. The technician was busy nearly all the time, either demonstrating the apparatus (the lecture happened to be on static electricity) or putting equations on the blackboard as they were called for by the tape. Professor Kirkpatrick had given him a list of equations to write on the board when they were wanted.

"The illusion was very good. It seemed just as though the technician were giving the lecture. It seemed as though he were using an amplifier so that his words came out of a loudspeaker—and everybody is used to that—while he demonstrated and wrote on the board. It really worked well.

"But in my opinion the illusion that made this taped lecture effective depended on the presence and activity of the real live technician. If the lecture had been on history, for instance, with no demonstrations and no equations on the blackboard, I think it would have failed to grip. If it had been on mathematics, with no demonstrations but plenty of equations to write on the board . . . I don't know. However, you will recognize the difference between this taped lecture in which the illusion is centered around a live technician and a film or television show with only a picture of a person.

"Now I can go back to Andrew's question—has such a movie actually been made? The answer is yes. I have seen a film made by the Mathematical Association of America—actually, a film under their auspices made in Hollywood by professionals—of Professor George Polya of our mathematics department teaching something about geometry to a group of students in a schoolroom. It is splendidly done; excellently presented and expertly filmed. It comes very close indeed to being the hypothetical movie that I was talking about a few minutes ago.

"The purpose of this film of Dr. Polya is to show how mathematics can be made interesting and effective for students of high school age, and this it certainly does. The students were real students and unrehearsed, and the geometry was genuinely new to them. The cameraman was clever; I most particularly remember seeing the face of an unsuspecting boy as the light dawned and his intent gaze on the blackboard was gradually replaced by a happy grin.

"Well, it is a marvelous picture, but still it is a picture. You are a delighted spectator, but you are not one of the students."

"Still," said James, "in this mathematics movie or in the physics demonstration, there isn't a real teacher, is there? There isn't anyone to know what you are doing and to talk to you and to answer your questions. There isn't somebody . . . somebody who cares."

"No," I agreed.

6
Students
are people

Professor Ralph Smith came cheerily into Room 308, and the bell rang as he closed the door behind him. He hardly needed an introduction, for the seminar knew him, knew that he was professor of electrical engineering. I mentioned that he was in charge of the academic work of the department, that he had previously been in charge of engineering at San Jose State College, and that he was an eminently successful author of engineering books.

Professor Smith sat at the front table with a "thank you" to me and a quick smile to the seminar. He looked around at the young men.

"Peter I know, and Andrew of course, and Thomas. Now, which of you is James? Yes. And Bartholomew? Yes. Your home is in Illinois, isn't it, Bartholomew?"

"Yes," said Bartholomew, taken by surprise. "Yes, it is. This is my first term here."

"I see. Right," said Professor Smith with a rapid glance at his list, "you graduated last June from Northwestern University, didn't you?" and he went from man to man in the group, relating new faces to names that he had obtained from me that morning. I knew that Professor Smith would recognize each young man by name from that time on; I had seen him use this engaging approach before. I greatly envied him his ability.

"I have a job here at the university," said Professor Smith when each man was happy at having been recognized, "and so have you. My job is to teach; your job is to learn. It is your job to say to yourself, 'What can I learn from this teacher?' It is my job to ask myself, 'How can I make the idea that is in my mind available to this particular student?'

"But always remember, both now when you are students and later when you become teachers, that a student must *want* to get something out of a course. Perhaps you can help him want to learn, but until the student *wants* to do his job the teacher *cannot* do his.

"You men in this room expect to become teachers. Good. It will then be your job to be sensitive to your students, sensitive to what each one needs, to what he wants, and to what he is. You will have a class of students, and they will be different from each other. They won't all respond in the same way. What you say or what you do will mean different things to different men.

"All people have different reactions, and what makes a 'good teacher' for one man doesn't at all make a good teacher for somebody else. Why, just look at this small seminar. There are only fifteen of you, and the mere fact that you are here shows that you have similar interests. But your homes are in many different states; you have graduated from many different colleges; your cultural, religious, and national backgrounds are all very different. How can the words of a teacher mean the same thing to all of you? If I talk about literature or politics or economics, what I say will be differently interpreted depending on your backgrounds. Even if I talk about science or engineering, you will hear me say different things.

"Any teacher is like Professor Wiener of MIT (the man of *Cybernetics* fame, you know) who remarked that 'I never know what I said until I find out what was heard.' "

Andrew seemed to be murmuring something under his breath, and Professor Smith paused. "What's that, Andrew?"

"Oh, nothing, sir. Just a sentence that the Associated Press had hung on the wall in their office at the Carson City state capitol. It said, '*We know you believe you understand what you think we said, but we are not sure ...*' (how did it go?) ... '*but we are not sure you realize that what you heard is not what we meant.*' Yes, that's it."

"Right," said Professor Smith. "Yes, I see. Well, a teacher has to do what the AP says it can't—he has to be sure the student understands what he really means."

"But I don't see how he can." Thomas was plaintive. "There seem to be so many things a teacher has to do. I doubt that I'll ever be any good at teaching. I wouldn't even know where to start—how can I learn?"

"Well," replied Professor Smith, "do you know how a doctor learns to perform an operation?"

"No, sir."

"It's like this. You find an excellent surgeon. You watch him operate. You watch his technique. You see what he does. You learn from watching him."

"I see," said Thomas, and subsided.

"Your students will not only have different backgrounds," continued Professor Smith, "but they will be headed in different ways. Some may turn out to be research men while others, with much the same undergraduate education, will work their way into management. Here on these sheets—help yourself to a copy—I show nine different functions. I call it *The Engineering Spectrum*, because I'm an engineer, but it could refer to any other applied science without much change."

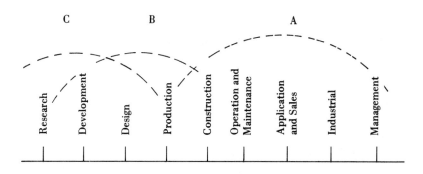

"You will find when you are teaching an engineering class that some of your students are certainly going to become professional engineers, the kind of engineers most people think about when engineers are mentioned. These men do design work. They are in charge of production, too, or construction if it happens to be that kind of business, and of course they are concerned with development; but their life work is characterized by design. These men come in the middle of the spectrum.

"A few of your students will be preparing for research, way over here at the left end of the spectrum. Naturally, engineering research isn't any use unless it leads to development and design and production, but nevertheless these men will have rather special interests.

"Then at the other end of the spectrum we find the large number of men who will operate the businesses, sell the goods, and manage the concerns. They have a real interest and ability in engineering (or at least we hope so, for they will need it) and they may have any title from superintendent to manager.

"So when you are teaching and advising students, which you will all do, remember this chart. It is not hard to tell which way a boy is headed, even when he is still quite young. If he likes to be with other people and do committee work and organize things, and if laboratory work is a necessary evil that unfortunately has got to be done, he will do well to look toward the function marked A in my spectrum.

"But if he likes to work in the lab where he can try things for himself, and he just hopes that people will go away and leave him alone, he will make a real success only in C."

"But sir," said Thomas, "surely a man's interests may change."

"Well, it is almost always true that a man's interests move a little from left to right in the spectrum, from science toward business, as he grows older. This we all know simply by watching our former students, and exceptions are quite rare. Apart from this gradual change with age a man does not shift much from one group to another.

"Of course there are a few fortunate boys who are interested in all the groups and who like to work in any of the functions, all the way from science at one end to management at the other. These boys will become the presidents of successful companies. Or teachers."

"Or teachers?" Thomas was startled.

"Yes. Consider your own interests. You like to work with people or you would not want to be a teacher. But you like the theory of subjects, too, for this is what teachers teach. So there you are; teachers like people, and they like abstract ideas, too."

"It still sounds pretty hard to me."

"What sounds hard, Thomas?"

"Well, knowing what your students are learning, and if they are learning what they ought to be learning, and all that."

"Yes, it *is* hard. You can tell a little about what they are learning from the questions they ask and from their answers to your quizzes or from homework. Another way that both Professor Vennard and I have found effective is to have a committee of students who meet with you now and then and tell you how things are going. They will tell you what their troubles are, and maybe you can decide what is wrong. Maybe you should give more examples in your lectures, or the class may not understand your mathematics, or perhaps you are calling for too much work or not enough. This feedback from a committee is especially helpful for simple things that you may not even know about but that bother the students. Possibly you write too small on the blackboard, or they can't hear you in the back of the room, or the air is hot and stuffy."

"But sir," asked James, "isn't there still a major problem if you have thirty students with thirty different backgrounds behind them and thirty different goals ahead of them?"

"There is, indeed. It is just this situation that takes all the understanding and skill that the teacher has.

"You ought to know each student personally as far as you can. The least you can do is to know his name and where he comes from. The more you can know about him the better. Remember that he is a person with ideas and ideals and an object in life. He has come from somewhere and, with your help, he is going somewhere.

"It is your job to guide him—to help him become a smarter student and a better engineer and a wiser man."

All are sleeping
just one is preaching:
Such performance is
called here "teaching."

7
Let us teach guessing

"In my class," said Professor Polya, "when I get the impression that I have spoken too long without interruption and should now ask a question of the students, I am apt to remember this jingle that I have approximately translated for you. It is German and has nothing to do with any American college—unless there is something universal about lectures."

I had introduced Professor Polya to my seminar as a teacher of mathematics and a mathematician. He had made contributions to mathematical analysis in several books and some 220 technical papers. He had been first at Zurich and then at Stanford, with shorter intervals as visiting scientist in England at Oxford and Cambridge and elsewhere in Europe. Now, on trips around the United States and Canada he was, he said, an "itinerant preacher of mathematics." He had contributed to good teaching through his travels and seminars; his books, *Mathematical Discovery*, *Mathematics and Plausible Reasoning*, the widely popular *How To Solve It*; and even a Hollywood movie produced by the Mathematical Association of America in which he demonstrated the teaching of mathematics to youngsters of high school age. I had intentionally toned down the introduction so that the seminar might not be overawed.

"I can give you no rules," began Professor Polya, "for there are as many good ways of teaching as there are good teachers. Teaching is not just a branch of applied psychology, at least not yet. The psychology of learning can give us many interesting hints, but the psychologists work best with simplified short-term situations, while we teachers are concerned with complex learning situations and their long-term educational effects.

"I have an old-fashioned idea about the aim of teaching. I believe the aim, first and foremost, is to teach young people to *think*. *Teaching to think* means that the teacher should not merely impart information, but should try to develop the ability to *use* this information. No doubt we can agree, whatever our opinions may be on the subject of teaching to think, that we do at least hope to develop the student's ability to solve problems.

"Socrates said that the teacher is midwife to the thought. Not parent, mark you, but midwife. The teacher does not have the thought; the student has the thought and the teacher helps it come.

"Now the hints that we get from the psychologists can be expressed as three principles of learning. These principles are by no means new. They are derived from the experience of the ages and are endorsed by the judgment of great men, as well as being suggested by the psychological study of learning.

"*Active learning*. Learning should be active, not merely passive or receptive. Merely by looking at television and moving pictures, listening to lectures, or reading books, you can hardly learn anything and certainly you cannot learn much without adding some action of your own mind. *The best way to learn anything is to discover it yourself.* This *Arbeitsprinzip* is very old. It underlies the Socratic method, and a reason was added two centuries ago by the physicist Lichtenberg who said, '*What you have been obliged to discover by yourself leaves a path in your mind which you can use again when the need arises.*'

"*Motivation*. Learning should be active, yet the student without a motive will not act. What will induce the student to make the necessary effort? Is there something the teacher can do? Simple interest in the subject is surely the best stimulus, and the pleasure of success in intensive mental activity should be the best reward. Yet there are other motives, such as future need for the material, and there are other rewards to be won, such as good grades or approval by the teacher and by others. (Punishment for not learning is perhaps the least desirable motive.)

"*Consecutive phases*. Let us consider *exploration*, *formalization*, and *assimilation*. I think you will have no trouble in recognizing these phases in some simple elementary material that you have learned or taught. After a while you may perceive similar phases in mastering more complex, more advanced material.

"A first *exploratory* phase is close to perception, and moves on an intuitive, heuristic level. A second *formalizing* phase ascends to a more conceptual level, introducing terminology, definitions, proofs. The phase of *assimilation* comes last: there should then be an attempt to understand the 'inner ground' of things. The material learned should be mentally digested and absorbed into the system of knowledge, into the whole mental outlook of the learner. This phase paves the way to applications on one hand and to higher generalizations on the other. Do you not recognize these three phases in something you yourself have learned?

"Now," said Dr. Polya, "Let us see how these three principles of learning lead to a teacher's ways of teaching. What can the teacher do to help the student to think? How can the teacher be midwife to the thought?

"Let me repeat for you an example that I might use to start a course in college mathematics. 'You all know about maps. You all use maps. You use road maps and maps of the world and maps of the United States. But what kind of a surface,' I ask, 'is a map?' And many in the class reply, 'A plane.' 'Yes,' I agree, 'and what is the earth?' And they say, 'A sphere.'

" 'Very well,' I say, 'at least as a first approximation we shall consider the earth to be a sphere.' I will then speak to the class of different projections, of which most will have heard, and we will talk about the meaning of a perfect map.

"Now I will ask *you*, please, to help in a little dialogue. I will take the part of the teacher of a beginning class in conformal mapping, and you will take the part of the class. So I will ask you, is it possible for a sphere to be mapped accurately on a plane surface? What do you guess? Answer, please, out loud so everybody can hear."

Several of the seminar saw what was wanted and replied more or less together, "No."

"Good. You have guessed. But can you prove it?"

This time there was no reply, until Thomas admitted, "I doubt it."

"Then," said Dr. Polya, "look," and he drew a circle on the blackboard. "This is a picture of a sphere, with points on its surface that I call A and B. Now here, next to it, is a plane map of the part of the surface that contains A and B. Points on the sphere map as points on the plane, lines map as lines and, if the map is to be perfect, then shortest lines must map as shortest lines, and angles between intersecting lines on the plane must be equal to angles between intersecting lines on the sphere.

"First, I shall assume that a perfect map is possible unless we can prove that it is not possible.

"Very well. Now what is the shortest path between points A and B on the plane? You all know? Yes, a straight line, of course. And what is the shortest path between points A and B on the sphere? Many will know: a great circle. Good. Let us draw a great circle on the sphere, and a straight line on the map. ·

"Now let us take another point C on the sphere, and by whatever projection we are using we put it also on the plane map. We connect it by great circles of the sphere to A and B, and if the map is perfect these great circles must map to straight lines on the plane—and I draw them.

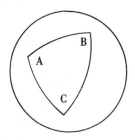 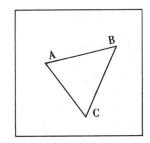

"Here on the plane we have a triangle ABC. Do you know what is the sum of the angles of a triangle? It is how much?"

This time the seminar were warming to the game and they all answered: "One hundred and eighty degrees."

"Good. Now here on the surface of the sphere we have a spherical triangle ABC. Does anyone know the sum of the angles?" But this time there was no answer.

"Very well," Dr. Polya continued, "then maybe you can tell me this: is it one hundred and eighty degrees?"

"No," James replied a little uncertainly, "it is more."

"That is right!" Dr. Polya was delighted. "The sum is more than one hundred and eighty degrees, and it is greater by an amount that is called in spherical geometry the *spherical excess*. You remember?"

The seminar tried to look as if they all thought they remembered.

"Yes, that is so. And now (I ask) can the angles on the sphere be mapped perfectly onto the plane?"

"No," the whole seminar answered together.

"You are right again. These three angles on the sphere cannot all be equal to these three on the plane. At least one and maybe all three must be different. Therefore, can the figure on the plane be a perfect map of the figure on the sphere?"

"No," they chorused.

"So, you see, now you have proved it. No matter what projection you use it is impossible to preserve both shortest distances and also angles in mapping a sphere onto a plane. Is it right?"

And the seminar answered, "Yes."

"Good. That is the end of our little play, which shows how I sometimes use this question about maps to start a discussion of mathematics. Now, why was this a good question? First, it is a natural problem. Everybody uses maps. Everybody is naturally interested in whether maps are right or not. It is possible that nearly everybody thinks he knows whether a map can be perfect, and he is willing and even anxious to guess, but nobody in the class can prove it one way or the other. Still, a proof is easy.

"When a boy guesses about the answer to a problem he has committed himself, and he is thereafter personally interested in the problem. He wants to see it proved that his guess is right, but he is still interested even if his guess was wrong. At least he cannot be indifferent for his prestige is at stake.

"At this point, let us look back at the three principles of learning. Has our teaching taken these principles into account?

"First, learning should be active. That is why we have worked so hard to get participation of the class in our problem. You will see that the class helped set up the problem in the first place: they helped decide that the earth will be considered a sphere and that the map is a plane, and they considered what is a perfect map. They furnished most of the facts from plane or spherical geometry. And they reached the conclusion of the proof, I hope, a little before I did. It is always best for the class to see the outcome of a problem just before it is announced by the teacher. Then they are very pleased with themselves, and so they like the subject.

"Second, the class will exert themselves to work on a problem only if they are interested, so what did we do? To begin with, we selected a problem that is naturally interesting. There is nothing worse than starting with a problem that interests nobody.

"Then we asked everybody in the class to give his opinion, and this helps keep them awake. We pretended to be very interested in the problem, too. You cannot always be excited about a proof that you have presented to a class many times before—but, please, do not show this to your class. If you appear bored, the whole class will be bored.

"This is one of the few certain rules in teaching: if the teacher is bored, everybody is bored," and it was here that Professor Polya recited the verse "All are sleeping, just one is preaching. . . ."

"So pretend to be excited about the proof when you start it, pretend to have bright ideas when you proceed, pretend to be surprised and elated when the proof ends. You should do a little acting for the sake of your students who occasionally may learn more from your attitudes than from the subject matter presented.

"The profession of the teacher has something in common with the profession of the actor. I must confess that I take pleasure in a little acting," and here Professor Polya looked so happy and smiling that it was impossible not to believe he was really having the time of his life.

"It is your duty as a teacher, as a salesman of knowledge, to convince the student that your subject *is* interesting, that the point just under discussion is interesting, that the problem he is supposed to do deserves his best effort. There are so many interesting things in the world around us that the lad who refuses to learn mathematics may be neither lazy nor stupid—perhaps he is just more interested in something else.

"Some matters are necessarily routine, of course, and yet must be learned. Everyone must know about minus b plus or minus the square root of b squared minus $4ac$ over $2a$, and it can be put to them that they will need it very often in all later work so they can save time by learning it now.

"But, please, when you are teaching a class, do not make any matter more dreary than it has to be. You know, of course, that a teacher should not say things just once but three or four times. Yet repeating the same sentence several times may be terribly boring and defeat its own purpose. Well, teaching has something in common with music, and you can learn from the composers how to do it better. One of the principal art forms of music is *air with variations*. Perhaps you can begin by saying your sentence in its simplest form; then you repeat it with a little change; then you repeat it again with still more color, and so on; and you may wind up by returning to the original simple formulation.

"Or, translating the *rondo* into teaching, you repeat the same essential sentence several times with little or no change, but you insert between repetitions some appropriately contrasting illustrative material. I hope that when you next listen to a theme with variations by Beethoven or to a rondo by Mozart you will give a little thought to improving your teaching.

"Third, the class will learn from the problem in *consecutive phases*. We encouraged first the exploratory phase, the intuitive phase, by encouraging guessing. In fact, in the work of a scientist, the guess almost always precedes the proof. This can be called heuristic investigation if you like. Thus, in letting the students guess the result, we not only motivate them to work harder, but we also teach them a desirable attitude of mind. Even in pure mathematics, progress is first suggested by informal thought processes, and precise formulation comes later. Let us teach proving by all means, but let us also teach guessing.

"After this exploratory phase comes the phase of formalization—the phase of proof. This is important. It is the time of putting ideas into symbols and words, of formulating definitions and proofs, and it must precede the final phase as the gathering of information must precede its use.

"Our knowledge about any subject consists of information and know-how. Know-how is the ability to use information. Know-how in mathematics is the ability to do problems and to recognize mathematical concepts in concrete situations. This comes in the final phase.

"In our student problem about maps and the globe we first guess an answer, and this guess—whether right or wrong—guides us toward a better understanding. We find the way in which to go, and the formal proof can then be pursued. These are phases one and two, and with a formal proof complete, the class is ready to proceed to phase three.

"In phase three we consider what to do with our newly acquired knowledge. Perhaps in this phase of assimilation we can show applications. A map is intended, let us say, for navigation, and it is desired that a ship follow a rhumb line. If the helmsman maintains a prescribed angle between the direction of the ship's course and the true north direction (which is shown by a suitably corrected compass), the ship proceeds along a line that intersects all meridians at the same angle, a *rhumb line*. The helmsman wishes to have the angle between the course of the ship and the meridian correctly represented on his map and, moreover, to have any rhumb line he may sail represented as a straight line on the map. Can this be done? Yes, it can be shown that the Mercator projection does so. But is a distance on the Mercator map proportional to a distance on the earth? Unfortunately, no; the scale of the map varies with the latitude. So the map is not perfect.

"Or perhaps a map is wanted that will show true distances and also true directions from a radio receiver to many distant transmitting stations; is there such a map? Yes; if you receive the signals always at just one place, there is the equiazimuth projection. But it centers on one point only.

"There are many projections, and many of them have advantages along with disadvantages. These suggest a number of new problems for a course that is concerned with mapping. One of the virtues of a good problem is that it generates other good problems.

"In one way or another the result of our problem must be related to what the students already know, and both the teacher and the students must contribute to this phase of digestion. Finally we accept the new knowledge, and we are then ready to pass on to some higher generalization that has perhaps already been suggested.

"But I remind myself of the German jingle. I have been preaching too long. I hope," said Professor Polya to the seminar, "that you have not already gone to sleep?"

They had not; indeed they had been amused and serious by turns. Andrew was obviously bursting with a question.

"Sir, you spoke of information and know-how. Do you mean that information is what a teaching machine can teach and know-how takes a real, actual teacher?"

Professor Polya was true to his principle of inviting participation. "Tell me, what do we mean by know-how?"

"Well, isn't it the ability to do problems? To use information? To see what questions you ought to ask? Something like that. . . . "

"So. And do you know of a machine that will guide you in decisions of this kind?"

"Well, no, sir. I don't think I know of a machine that will do this kind of teaching. Can there really be such a machine?"

"You should invent one. It would be a great thing."

"But there are such machines already," put in James. "At least I think there are—aren't there?"

"You know of a machine that will teach the student to think? That is very good. Everybody demands that the schools should impart to the students not only information but know-how, independence, originality, creativity."

"Creativity," repeated Peter. "Is creativity the same as solving problems?"

"Creativity is perhaps something more than the solution of a routine problem. But not all problems are routine. A good problem first requires some mental activity in setting up the problem and even in seeing that there *is* a problem. Then it requires some degree of concentration and judgment—and, to that degree, its solution is *creative*. In research it is often more difficult to put the problem than to answer it, and a classroom problem may sometimes approach the research level."

"I'd like to be a teacher," said Thomas unhappily, "but I just know that I can't do all these things that you tell us a good teacher ought to do. Isn't there some easier way?"

"The important things are not easy. You must be interested in your subject. You must remember that learning is active and lead your students to guess. You must put yourself in their place and try to see their expectations and their difficulties. That is the very least."

"I can ask questions of a class, but I don't think I can get them to answer," grieved Thomas. "I *have* tried a little teaching, but when I ask a question, nothing happens."

"Don't ask 'em," advised Matthew. "Tell 'em."

"Oh, please." Professor Polya was pained. "A teacher must be infinitely patient. Suggest it; do not force it down their throats. Try to avoid saying 'you are wrong'. Say instead, if possible, 'you are right, but. . . . ' If you say too often 'that is wrong', the students will hate you and your subject, and all interest and learning will be gone."

"I tell them all the interesting things I can," sighed Thomas, "but I doubt if they pay any attention."

"Oh, but do not give away your whole secret at once." Professor Polya was smiling again, perhaps amused by the doleful Thomas. "Let the students guess before you tell it. Remember what Voltaire said, that I translate very roughly: 'The secret of being tiresome is to tell all.' "

8

Lectures became obsolete

Andrew was already sitting in Room 308 when I came in on the following Thursday afternoon. He was gazing at a stack of paper in front of him with a curious expression. It was almost as if he wanted to be disturbed. He continued to gaze at the stack of folded paper as I sat opposite him. Peter and John and a few others of the seminar wandered into the room.

I arranged my notebook and papers and finally asked, "What is all that, Andrew?"

"Gosh, sir, I don't know. A friend of mine got it out of the computer."

"Out of a computer? That?"

"Yes, sir. So my friend told me, sir. He said he went around with a problem for the computer just as he always does, but when he got the print-out from the machine this is what came out."

"Well, what is it?"

"I don't know if I ought to show you, sir." Andrew seemed doubtful and this intrigued me, as I suppose he knew it would. I moved to see what he had, and he rather hesitantly pushed over to me a typical computer print-out. However, instead of the usual array of numbers with a few words of explanatory writing, I could see only page after page of text. It was all in capitals, of course, for the machine has no other letters, and Andrew's sheet began with the heading LECTURES BECAME OBSO-LETE.

I read on. Peter and John watched for a moment and then came to read

read over our shoulders. Presently a bell rang to mark the beginning of the seminar hour. The others had arrived and were watching curiously. Clearly this could not go on. I said to Andrew, "I don't believe a word of what you say, but there's nothing else to do; you'll have to read this thing to the seminar."

"Oh, no, sir."

"Andrew!"

"Must I, sir?"

"Yes," I said, "you must."

"Well . . . very well, sir."

I strongly suspected that this was what Andrew had planned, but in a few words of explanation to the seminar I merely acquiesced in Andrew's account of his friend and the computer, and he read aloud:

IT HAS BEEN SAID BY SOME THOUGHTLESS PERSON, PERHAPS WELL-MEANING BUT SURELY WITHOUT UNDERSTANDING, THAT LECTURES BECAME OBSOLETE WHEN THE PRINTING PRESS WAS INVENTED. SINCE THIS DEPLORABLE STATEMENT SHOWS A LACK OF APPRECIATION OF THE FINER SHADES OF ACADEMIC LIFE AND AN ABSENCE OF TRUE SENSITIVITY, IT BECOMES A DUTY TO REFUTE SO SLANDEROUS A PRO-NOUNCEMENT.

IN THE EARLY MIDDLE AGES WHEN UNIVERSITIES FIRST APPEARED, THE FINE TECHNIQUE OF THE LECTURE SYSTEM WAS DEVELOPED. IN ITS CLASSIC FORM, THE LECTURER, GUIDED AND INSPIRED BY HIS OWN NOTEBOOK, SPOKE TO A CLASS OF YOUNG MEN WHO RAPIDLY SET DOWN ON PAPER AS MANY OF THE PROFESSOR'S WORDS AS POSSIBLE. THUS AT THE END OF A COURSE OF LECTURES IT RESULTED THAT EACH STUDENT HAD PRODUCED FOR HIMSELF A REASONABLE REP-LICA OF THE PROFESSOR'S NOTEBOOK, AND ONE SET OF NOTES HAD BECOME MANY. THIS PROCESS CAME TO BE CALLED THE "PROPAGA-TION OF KNOWLEDGE."

FROM ITS VERY BEGINNING THE LECTURE SYSTEM BROUGHT JOY TO THE PROFESSOR. WHAT COULD BE MORE DELIGHTFUL THAN GIVING A SERIES OF WELL ORGANIZED AND NICELY PRESENTED LECTURES, PRE-PARING ONE'S IDEAS IN A CAREFULLY ARRANGED AND WHOLLY LOG-ICAL ORDER AND THEN DELIVERING THEM WITH JUST THE RIGHT AMOUNT OF ORATORICAL EMBELLISHMENT, LIGHTENED BY A FEW OF THE HUMOROUS TOUCHES THAT GIVE SO MUCH PLEASURE? THE RE-SULT IS DELIGHTFUL, AND THE PROFESSOR IS THE MORE CERTAINLY ASSURED OF SATISFACTION IF HIS AUDIENCE COMES OF NECESSITY, LISTENS THROUGH APPREHENSION OF EXAMINATION, AND LAUGHS (ALWAYS AT THE RIGHT PLACES) BY VIRTUE OF GOOD JUDGMENT.

YET FOR THE MEDIEVAL STUDENTS THIS LUTE WAS NOT WITHOUT ITS RIFT. EARNEST YOUNG MEN WOULD BE FOUND DAY AFTER DAY AT NARROW DESKS WITH QUILLS FLYING BETWEEN INK-POT AND PAPER

AS THEY SOUGHT TO TRANSCRIBE THE PROFESSOR'S WORDS, AND THE SIMPLE BEAUTY OF THE SYSTEM SEEMED TO SOME OF THEM INADEQUATELY TO COMPENSATE FOR THE TEDIOUSNESS OF TRANSCRIPTION. FOR MANY A STUDENT IT WAS SUFFICIENT COMFORT TO KNOW, WHEN THE BOOK WAS CLOSED AT THE END OF THE LAST LECTURE, THAT HERE BETWEEN HIS OWN COVERS LAY THE WISDOM OF THE PROFESSOR SHOULD IT EVER BE WANTED, BUT OTHERS WERE DISTURBED BY A SHADOWY REGRET THAT THE SPEED OF WRITING LEFT LITTLE TIME FOR UNDERSTANDING. COULD IT HAVE BEEN IN A RESULTING MOMENT OF FRUSTRATION THAT THERE WAS COINED THAT FOOLISH ADAGE IN WHICH THE LECTURE SYSTEM IS CENSURED AS BEING THE MEANS BY WHICH NOTES ARE TRANSFERRED FROM THE BOOK OF THE LECTURER TO THAT OF THE STUDENT WITHOUT PASSING THROUGH THE MINDS OF EITHER? BUT THIS IS BEST FORGOTTEN.

WHEN, IN COURSE OF TIME, IT CAME ABOUT THAT THE PRINTING PRESS WAS INVENTED AND BOOKS APPEARED, IT SEEMED THAT A CHANGE MIGHT BE PORTENDED IN THE LECTURE SYSTEM OF THE UNIVERSITIES. PRAY CONSIDER THE POSSIBILITY. WOULD THE PROFESSOR NOW ABANDON HIS LECTURE? COULD THE STUDENT NOW AVOID THE ETERNAL DRUDGERY OF TRANSCRIPTION?

AS TO THE FORMER, NO; CERTAINLY NOT. THE PROFESSOR COULD HARDLY BE EXPECTED TO CAST AWAY HIS OPPORTUNITY TO APPEAR AS THE WISE MENTOR CONFERRING UPON BRIGHT YOUNG MINDS THE WINNOWED WISDOM OF GENERATIONS. BY NO MEANS; THE LECTURES WOULD PROCEED.

BUT AS TO THE LATTER, THE WRETCHED PLIGHT OF THE TRANSCRIBING STUDENTS WAS SOON TO BE RELIEVED, FOR IT WAS DISCOVERED THAT THEIR INKY DRUDGERY COULD NOW BE RELEGATED TO THE PRINTING PRESS, AND AS THE PASSING CENTURIES BROUGHT THIS REALIZATION TO PROFESSORS AS WELL AS STUDENTS WE SAW, OR SEE, THE PASSING OF WHAT MAY BE CALLED THE "ARCHETYPAL LECTURE SYSTEM."

RELIEF THUS CAME, OR COMES, TO THE STUDENTS IN RETURN FOR A MODEST EXPENDITURE AT THE BOOKSTORE, AND THE CHANGE IS NOT ONLY PERMITTED BUT EVEN ENCOURAGED BY THE PROFESSOR BECAUSE A NEW STAR HAS APPEARED IN HIS HEAVENS ALSO. THE GATES OF AUTHORSHIP HAVE OPENED BEFORE HIM, FOR WHO IF NOT HIMSELF WOULD WRITE THE BOOKS TO BE PURCHASED BY HIS STUDENTS? SOME EXTRAMURAL PROFESSOR MIGHT INDEED WRITE A BOOK ON THE SAME SUBJECT, AND PERHAPS THE USE OF SUCH A SUBSTITUTE MIGHT SERVE TEMPORARILY WHILE THE PROFESSOR COMPOSED HIS OWN WORK, BUT THIS WOULD BE A STOPGAP ONLY. THE PROFESSOR'S OWN BOOK WOULD BE PUBLISHED SHORTLY.

DID THIS PROVISION OF THE PROFESSOR'S WISDOM IN PRINT MEAN THAT HIS LECTURES WOULD BE CURTAILED? NOT AT ALL. THE LECTURES WOULD CONTINUE AS USUAL, FOR IF THE HOUR IN WHICH A PROFESSOR STOOD BEFORE HIS CLASS WERE NOT DEVOTED TO A

PLEASING LECTURE DELIVERED DECENTLY AND IN ORDER, TO WHAT OCCUPATION SHOULD THIS FIFTY MINUTES BE DEVOTED? IF THESE MOMENTS WERE NOT OCCUPIED BY A SUITABLE AND PROPER LECTURE, SOME RUDE, UNSTRUCTURED FORM OF ACTION MIGHT ERUPT. STUDENT VOICES MIGHT BE HEARD ASKING QUESTIONS, EVEN EMBARRASSING QUESTIONS ABOUT EXAMPLES AND PROBLEMS FROM THE LIFE AROUND US—AND SURELY HERE LIES ANARCHY. NO; THE LECTURE MUST GO ON!

WITH THESE CONSIDERATIONS THE UNIVERSITY HAS NOW COME, IN ITS WISDOM, TO THE PLAN BY WHICH EVERYONE IS MADE HAPPY, THE MODERN BILATERAL LECTURE SYSTEM. WITHOUT IN ANY WAY CURTAILING THE LECTURES THE WRITTEN WORD HAS BEEN ADDED TO THE SPOKEN WORD, AND THE STUDENT NOW REJOICES IN BOTH. WE HAVE THE LECTURES AND WE HAVE THE BOOKS ALSO.

A CERTAIN DIFFICULTY HAS APPEARED, IT IS SAID, IN THIS GREAT BILATERAL PLAN. IT IS ONLY NATURAL THAT THE PROFESSOR'S LECTURES SHOULD OFTEN CONTAIN MATERIAL SIMILAR TO THAT OF THE PRINTED BOOK, AND THIS IS PARTICULARLY LIKELY IF THE LECTURER WAS HIMSELF THE AUTHOR. SHOULD WE NOW SUPPOSE THE STUDENTS TO HAVE READ THE BOOK BEFORE COMING TO CLASS, AND THIS THEY MAY EVEN HAVE BEEN DIRECTED TO DO, IT WILL HARDLY BE SURPRISING IF, DESPITE THEIR BEST EFFORTS, THEY SOMETIMES FAIL IN ENTHUSIASM WHEN THE JOKES OF THE BOOK REAPPEAR IN THE LECTURE. TO THIS EXTENT, THEN, THE BEST OF LECTURERS MAY MEET DIAPPOINTMENT; IT SEEMS INEVITABLE.

BUT ON THE OTHER HAND THE BILATERAL PLAN PROVIDES FOR AN ESSENTIAL NEED OF THE STUDENTS. I DO NOT SPEAK OF THE PRESENT DAY ALONE BUT OF A REQUIREMENT OF THE YOUNG PERSON *IN STATU PUPILLARI* THROUGH THE AGES. WHAT A BOON IT MUST HAVE BEEN TO THE HARD WORKING STUDENT WHEN THE BILATERAL PLAN WAS ACHIEVED AND HE FOUND HIMSELF THE BENEFICIARY IN AN UNPREMEDITATED WAY. HE COULD NOW, UNDER THIS SPLENDID NEW SYSTEM OF LECTURE *AND* BOOK, ACTUALLY DEVOTE ANOTHER CLASSROOM HOUR TO SLEEP. THAT FINEST OF ALL THINGS, SLEEP.

THUS WE SEE UPHELD THE GLORY OF THE UNIVERSITY, WHICH CAN AND DOES REJOICE IN ITS GREAT LECTURERS AND IN ITS FAMOUS AUTHORS AND IN ITS BRILLIANT STUDENTS. THE UNIVERSITY LECTURERS CAN STILL BE HAPPY IN THEIR LECTURES. THE AUTHORS CAN NOW BE HAPPY IN THEIR BOOKS. AND THE STUDENTS CAN BE HAPPY—IN SLEEP.

Andrew stopped.

"Andrew," I said, "where did you really get that?"

"Why, it came out of the computer, and my friend, Warren Wonka, gave it to me."

"Don't you realize that it is subversive?"

"No," he said. "Is it?"

"Burn it, Andrew," I advised. "Burn it before something worse happens."

9

Feedback

Professor Franklin, listening to my introduction, looked at the seminar with a slow, amiable grin, for the introduction was not going well.

"It is only natural for Professor Franklin to think of an instructor and a class as parts of a feedback system, for feedback systems are his special subject. As you know, he heads the group of our department people who are working on systems; he has written a book and any number of papers and reports on the subject, so of course he sees a teacher and his students as devices in an educational feedback network. . . . " This sounded good and perhaps it would have been an adequate introduction for someone else, but for Gene Franklin it quite missed; it seemed to suggest something impersonal or mechanical, and I am afraid that those of the seminar who knew Professor Franklin at all well were amused. So I gave up the introduction and just asked Professor Franklin to take over.

"It is surely true that education is a form of feedback system." Professor Franklin's pleasant voice suggested the South. "Education is a sampled-data feedback system. Education is an adaptive feedback system, too, or so we hope, for we trust that the teacher as well as the students will be capable of learning.

"I expect I should start by putting a block diagram on the board because that is what we always do when we talk about systems. We'll begin here at the left. Here is where the reference signal comes in, from this block that represents the book or syllabus or whatever it is that defines the course. The reference signal is fed in to the instructor—so. Maybe it is fed in to the class directly, too—maybe they have copies of the book or syllabus—so I'll draw this line across the top."

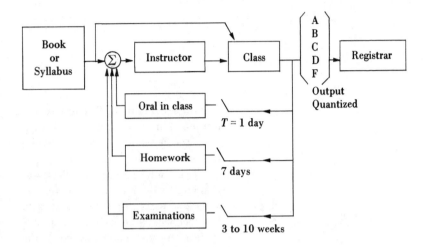

"Here we have the class, and this is the students' output. I'll draw just one line to represent the output of all the students. Each student's output is then quantized as A, B, C, D, F, or perhaps 0 to 100 percent, and at the end of the term the quantized results are transmitted to the registrar.

"Now here are feedback paths from the class to the instructor. The students' output can appear as examination papers, as written homework, or as oral questions and comments in class, and the feedback comes around here from *class* output to *instructor* input by way of this little circle with a Σ in it called a summing device.

"But feedback is not continuous. You can get oral feedback whenever the class is in session, but written homework is intermittent and may come only once a week or so, and regular examinations are given at intervals of several weeks. All this feedback is a kind of sampled data, for you get samples only at certain times.

"In my diagram I can show switches in the circuits. This top switch is for 'oral response in class' and we close it every day the class meets. The next one, for homework, takes a sample once a week, and so on.

"But then each feedback path has a time constant. Let's say the instructor collects the written work on Friday, but he doesn't know the results until the following Wednesday. Maybe the papers are lying on his desk or maybe a corrector has them. This means that after the sample is taken there's a delay before the feedback reaches the instructor. I suppose that for oral feedback in class there isn't really any delay and the time constant of that channel is negligible; but for written work, and even more for examinations, the time constant is apt to be several days at least.

"Then we have to consider that some feedback channels give stronger signals than others and more feedback gets through to the instructor. Let's look at two extremes of designing feedback channels.

"One extreme we can call Method 1. This gives strong feedback. All written work, everything, is graded by the teacher, and he uses the results to modify his lectures and other class material. This is a good system but it's a lot of hard work for the teacher.

"The other extreme is Method 2. All class papers are read and graded by an assistant. The instructor doesn't even look at the papers himself but only sees the grades. Feedback is very weak; in fact there is so much attenuation in the channel that hardly any feedback gets through at all.

"I suppose most teachers actually use some kind of a compromise between Method 1 and Method 2. The teacher always does the detailed design of his own educational system, but some general design criteria are generally imposed from above in the form of instructions about how he is to do his job.

"It is usual, of course, for the designer of any system to have to meet specifications, and his responsibility is to design the best possible system within those specifications. He probably has to devise a system with a good *speed of response* and a good *steady-state accuracy*. In our educational feedback system we can get a good speed of response from what the students say in class and from their answers to questions. On the other hand, we get good accuracy but slow results from written homework and formal written examinations. The best system design certainly includes some of both kinds of feedback.

"I'm afraid it's true that some lecturers don't encourage any oral response from their classes. They say that classes are too large or there isn't time. Well, they have eliminated the quick feedback channel and so they have to get along with a less responsive system. If the class is having trouble the instructor won't know about it until the homework is corrected; with a sampling period of seven days and a time constant of five days more, it could be a long time before the instructor had a chance to react.

"Maybe some instructors don't even require homework to be turned in, and then trouble won't appear in the feedback until an examination is given. This can mean a sampling period of five weeks or more, and with a further delay on top of that, it is possible for the course to be all over before the instructor finds out that his excellent lectures meant very little to the class. By that time it is forever too late; for that class at least all feedback had been eliminated.

"We learn from system theory that the way to have a responsive system that stays on the target and doesn't waste time is to have quick, strong feedback. Would I propose giving a short quiz in class every day, with the papers corrected by the instructor that same afternoon? Well, I think there are reasons why a quiz a day wouldn't always be a good idea, but the feedback would surely be quick and strong; whether a system is electrical, mechanical, educational, quick strong feedback keeps it on target.

"Now," said Professor Franklin, "I've talked a good deal about feedback and I think it's time for me to stop and invite a little feedback from you. What about it?"

The seminar was silent for a while, thinking it over. Finally Philip confessed, "I'm afraid I never thought of an instructor changing his lectures because of what the homework showed."

"Yes," said Professor Franklin. "Feedback."

"But surely there are other reasons for homework?"

"Oh, yes. Lots of them. Practice and drill; learning by doing. Practical applications. Specific use of general ideas. These are values the student can get from doing homework problems even if he doesn't turn them in. When he brings them back to the instructor they become feedback, and then there are several more values: First, the teacher can evaluate his own work by finding what the class has learned from him. Second, he can evaluate the book or syllabus of the course (way out here on the extreme left of my diagram). Third, he can evaluate the students' performance, getting grades to report to the registrar. Fourth, each student can evaluate his own achievement from the corrections and grades on the papers. He can tell how well he is doing and maybe find ways in which he can do better."

After a moment Bartholomew, who was often interested in examinations, remarked, "Written examinations are a slow kind of feedback, aren't they? Oral exams would be much faster."

"I guess oral examinations do have a negligible time constant."

"But," protested Matthew, "oral examinations aren't very fair."

"Wel-l, that depends. They *can* be fair. It is harder to compare the work of one student with that of another in an oral exam, but you can find out a lot about how much a man knows. The teacher who gives an oral examination needs to be good at it or he can waste a lot of time, but that's true of any examination, written or oral. The questions in an oral examination ought to be quite different from written examination questions, and the examiner should hardly ever wait for a complete answer. But on the whole they can be quite fair, I think. They work very well to rank a class from first to last in order of performance."

"But oral exams don't give you any absolute scale of grades, do they?" Thomas had come up through the military academy.

"No, I don't suppose so, but I wonder what an absolute scale of grades could mean anyway."

"Why, what percentage you know, and what percentage of questions you can answer."

"It seems to me that how many questions you can answer depends on how hard the questions are. Maybe you can be graded as doing better or worse than somebody else, but I can't see how anyone can devise an examination to give an absolute scale, really. Maybe a teacher can compare a student with everybody in the same year, or with everybody in several years, or even with every student he has ever known. Is that what you mean by an absolute scale?"

"No," Thomas said, "I mean more than that. I mean . . . I mean. . . . "

"I've often heard about an absolute scale," said Professor Franklin, "but I just can't believe there is any such thing."

Thomas looked unhappy. He had been brought up to believe in an absolute scale and a change came hard. However, he had nothing to say.

Bartholomew raised his hand. "They gave me a 'take-home' exam last term," he said, "and I think take-home exams are miserable."

"It seems to me," added James, "that take-home exams are not only unfair to me, but they take time away from the work I ought to be doing for other courses."

"I hate them," said John, agreeing with his brother for almost the first time that year.

"So do I," agreed Philip, and heads nodded around the seminar.

"Well, I have to agree with you," said Professor Franklin. "If what is meant by a take-home exam is an examination that you write out of class, by yourself at home, and then turn in to the instructor as if it were a regular examination paper. There seem to be two kinds: those with a time limit and those without.

"If there *is* a time limit and the student is supposed to limit his own work, it puts an awful strain on the student. Besides, I don't know why it's any better than a regular examination in class. You know, I could almost sympathize with a student who sort of forgot to watch the clock when he was supposed to be timing himself on an exam at home. It seems to me it's just too much of a strain, and I wouldn't want to give that kind of examination myself.

"But if there is *no* time limit except that you are given the take-home exam on Monday and it has to be turned in on the following Wednesday, there's a strain of a different kind. You know your grade in the course is going to depend on how well you do on that paper, and you know that all the other students in the class are going to be working day and night on that take-home exam—or at least you think they are and that's just as bad—so you feel that you have just got to spend two days and nights on the thing. This comes right in the middle of examination week, too, so you can't prepare properly for other course examinations, and you can't even get a decent amount of sleep. It's not only unfair to the students; it's unfair to other teachers. I wouldn't want to give that kind of an examination either."

"These take-home exams aren't always given during exam week," suggested Peter.

"Oh, well then, that's another matter. In that case we wouldn't have to call them take-home exams. We could just call them term problems or something, and they wouldn't be so worrying. I wouldn't object to an assignment like that, if it wasn't stressed too much. A term problem can fit in nicely with other homework and with quizzes and examinations to determine a grade for a course."

"You can learn something from a term problem, too," Andrew remarked. "It can be a practical kind of problem and not just a lot of fiddley little questions such as those in examinations."

"Yes," agreed Professor Franklin, "but you can learn from an examination, too, if it is well designed. Students are very receptive at examination time, and a teacher is wasting an opportunity if his examination doesn't teach as well as test. It's one of those things that you have to learn to do by trying, like so much of the business of teaching."

"If a teacher tries one method of teaching," asked Philip, "and that way doesn't give very good results. . . . "

"Yes?"

"So then he tries another method, and the results get better. . . . "

"Yes."

"And he keeps on trying, and changing his way of teaching. . . . "

"Well?"

"Is that what you'd call an *adaptive* feedback system?"

"Yes, that's it. If the teacher learns by teaching to do a better job, he's adapting. And that's the way you have to learn to teach, because nobody has good teaching built into him. A violinist has to practice and hear the result and improve. A teacher has to teach and get feedback from his class and improve. He has to be an adaptive element in his educational feedback system, because he is surely not born with good teaching designed into his structure.

"Let this be a lesson to you, Philip. When you start teaching, your class will be learning. But you'll be learning, too. You'll be learning how to teach, and you'll be adapting to the feedback you get. You'll adapt fast, because one thing we know about adaptive systems is that they improve very rapidly at first. So when you start teaching a class, Philip, remember that, if you want to be part of a really high-class educational feedback system, it's up to you to make yourself a good adaptive device."

10

Breathing down your neck

The next meeting of the seminar was on a rainy spring day. Peter folded an umbrella as he came in, and James shook a few drops of water from his raincoat. Mr. D. I. Cone, who sometimes joined our seminar because of his interest in teaching, sat at one side of the room. Matthew tucked his damp coat under a chair and came up to me.

"I want to say some more about examinations," he stated somewhat crossly.

"All right," I agreed. "What is wrong with examinations?"

"The way some instructors give them is all wrong. There isn't time to finish and they don't show what a man knows and there are too many questions and they aren't fair." Matthew was a little incoherent.

"I see." The seminar had now found seats and was turning to listen to Matthew, so I spoke to the room generally. "Matthew has suggested a little more consideration of examinations, and I suppose we might all be interested in continuing last week's discussion for awhile. Matthew feels, I think, that examinations aren't always fair. Did you have an examination today, Matthew?"

"Yes," said Matthew shortly. He had gone back to his seat.

"What was wrong with it?"

"Well, there just wasn't any time to think. Everybody needed another hour, but the professor collected the papers and we didn't have nearly time enough."

"I had one like that yesterday," said James. The week of midterm examinations was in full swing. "I never got to the last question at all."

"Maybe you didn't, but I finished it all," John commented.

"Did you?" said James. "Did you get it right?"

It seemed to me to be time to change the subject, so I asked of the seminar at large, "What about examinations, anyway? Are they always too long?"

"I like them long," said Philip. "Then if you can't answer one question maybe you can do another."

"The trouble is," said Matthew, reverting to his grievance, "they put you under pressure. This isn't a fair test, for lots of fellows could do better if they didn't feel that the paper was going to be snatched away from them in a few minutes."

"When you get out of school and you're working on a job you have time to do it," put in James.

But Andrew said, "Oh, golly, do you think so? When I was working for Edam Electronics they sure gave me lots of jobs that wanted an answer of some kind right quick. Generally about yesterday," he added.

"I don't think they ought to do that," said James. "How can a company expect you to give them the right answer if you don't have time to work on it?"

"There just wouldn't *be* that much time," said John. "Not for *you* to get the right answer."

Again I felt the time had come to interrupt. "Well," I remarked, "you all know Mr. Cone here, who joins us sometimes. He was in charge of an engineering department of the telephone company, and maybe he will tell us if there really is pressure to get an answer when you are on a job?"

"Yes, indeed," said Mr. Cone, and you could tell that he spoke with conviction. "There certainly is a time limit on most jobs. Sometimes a job has to be finished, and you have to get it done regardless of anything.

"The company might be getting ready for a commission hearing, or the specifications for a new plant might have to be finished. A man often has to turn out a lot of work in quick time."

"There is likely to be a deadline that an engineer has to have in mind as he works?"

"There is indeed," Mr. Cone said dryly.

"Which is the better man," I asked at large, "a man who can do a certain job if he has plenty of time or a man who can do the same job in less time?"

"Oh, but that isn't a fair question," objected James. "The first man might do the best job by taking more time."

"But a quick answer is what the company pays you a salary for," put in Andrew. "They don't want a treatise next week; they want the right answer today."

"This is sometimes true," Mr. Cone agreed, "but not always. Some problems require a long and detailed study, and I have found that the higher management people are very human and understanding about allowing time when it is necessary.

"All kinds of demands come along, and you can put them in a spectrum, from those that require an immediate response (at one end of the spectrum), through those that need an order-of-magnitude answer, to problems that take a careful study of all that is known on the subject and perhaps need further work in a physics laboratory, too.

"I really ought to emphasize the importance and value of an order-of-magnitude analysis. Perhaps the best answer you can give to a question is only approximate, and you know that your answer may be off by as much as three times, one way or the other. Still, such an answer can be very helpful. If something must happen in a millisecond, for instance, and your quick analysis shows that a proposed method will take something of the order of a second, you might just as well forget about that proposal.

"Then there are a good many questions that have no simple right answer. For instance, how will people feel about this or that? It is hard to say, but somebody has to guess. One thing clear is that the best man to answer one kind of question is not necessarily the best for another. It is the business of management to try to get square pegs into square holes."

"To get a good impedance match," suggested Andrew, "between the man and his job?"

"Yes," agreed Mr. Cone.

"Here," I said, hunting in my notebook. "Let me read you parts of this clipping by a man named Gorton. This is from a letter written several years ago to the Journal of Engineering Education by E. A. Gorton, Development Engineer for Pratt and Whitney Aircraft in Connecticut. He says:*

My concern is with the fate in industry of the engineering graduate who has been educated in an institution using the "no time limit" theory of examinations. Very soon after graduation he is most likely to

*Journal of Engineering Education, Vol. 50, No. 1, October 1959.

face an engineering task which even the most rapid and able of his examination-taking classmates would be unable to "finish" in the time allotted. Yet the best possible engineering answer must be provided [by the graduate], with all his superiors breathing down his neck, in a manner quite superior to that achieved by most college examiners. If our recently graduated friend has during his college career not been required to turn out his jobs under pressure of a time limit, how is he to react to a greater pressure in many industrial problems?

In practice it is seldom that the solution of engineering problems can be carried to perfection. . . .

There are no doubt many jobs where the pressure of time is not a large factor. If we wish to improve the examination as a measuring tool, it could be arranged that the student would face both "time unlimited" examinations and severely time limited examinations. . . . Those who panic under pressure could then at the start of their career be guided toward jobs tolerating that characteristic.

Well now," I asked, "What about that? First, Mr. Cone, you know about the industrial situation. What do you say?"

"Excellent," he replied.

"Other comments?"

"That's just what I think, too," said Andrew.

"Still," Matthew stuck to his guns, "I don't think it's fair."

"That," Andrew suggested, "depends on what you mean by 'fair'."

"The word 'fair'," I interposed didactically, "is difficult to define. Like the dangerous word 'ought' it implies a condition on which there may be lack of agreement."

This assertion rather stopped the discussion, and when we got under way again the subject had shifted to the differing requirements of "open book" and "closed book" examinations.

"I suppose you have to have a time limit on an open book examination," said Philip.

"What do you mean, open book?" asked Bartholomew, who was in his first term with us and had not yet learned all our peculiar ways.

"Why, an exam in which you can refer to your book or notes and things if you want," Philip explained.

"Do you mean you can look in the book during the examination?"

"Yes—or notes or anything. I like an open book exam, myself. It's a test of what you can do and not just a test of memory."

"Well," asked Bartholomew, "is that the kind of exam you have here? I haven't had any exams yet."

"Oh, we have both," said Philip. "It depends on the teacher."

"What I think," said Matthew, "is that some teachers give closed book exams just because it's easier to correct them. Isn't that right, sir?"

"Well," I admitted, "closed book examinations are certainly easier to correct. Still, there are probably some subjects in which the memory requirement of the closed book examination is a good thing. In elementary calculus, for instance, there are a number of formulas that you will need so often that it will save you time in the end if you just learn them by memory. For instance, you have to know that the derivative of the sine is the cosine and things like that." Even Matthew nodded agreement.

"But surely I could do very well in an examination if I could look up anything I needed to know, couldn't I?" wondered Bartholomew. "Don't the papers all come in nearly perfect?"

"No," said Philip, "because of time. You don't have time to look up very much and still finish."

"You can't ask anybody any questions?"

"Oh, no. That's the one thing you can't do. You can't ask anybody anything. You're on your own."

"One thing about open book exams, you can't cheat," added the practical Andrew. "You can't look at anything you're not supposed to, because there isn't anything you're not supposed to. And if you try asking anybody anything they won't tell you anyhow."

"Andrew's statement," I said, "is perhaps a trifle enigmatic, but the idea is quite correct. It really is almost impossible to cheat in an open book examination. However, as Philip says, there must be a strong time pressure for an open book examination to work well, and this means that it is harder for the instructor to make up the questions. Then, too, as Matthew said a minute ago, it is harder to correct an open book examination. All together, an open book examination is harder for the instructor to give."

"It does measure better, though, doesn't it sir?" urged Philip.

"Well," I tried to be impartial, "I suppose it depends on what you want to measure. I agree that I personally like an open book examination, but maybe it's because the courses I give are open book kinds of courses. I think the students generally like open book examinations better, too. And they are, I suppose, more like real life. Still, I must say that some perfectly sincere teachers like closed book examinations."

"I'll bet I know why," breathed Matthew.

11

Seeing is better

The next Thursday was bright between scattered clouds as we helped Professor Reynolds carry projectors and screens into Room 308. He had prepared a demonstration for us, a demonstration in three parts, showing some of the devices that we teachers in our technical jargon call "visual aids."

Professor William Reynolds, from the thermosciences faculty, would himself be part of his demonstration, for he was to enact the role of the teacher in his three one-act dramas.

In the first demonstration the seminar was to imagine itself a class in thermodynamics, listening to Professor Reynolds lecture on—whatever it was—but that made no difference—something about jet engines. The excellence of the blackboard was his real subject as he drew profiles of jet flow and diagrams and graphs in chalk of many colors, all of which he had carefully planned. One color was for the subsonic domain in equations and charts and graphs, and another for the supersonic. Most of us couldn't have known less about jet engine flow, but we saw jets and engines appear before us on the board in a neat, clear, swift, vigorous presentation.

The *chalkboard* (as one should say in these days when blackboards are not black) is an unsurpassed visual aid for illustrating a lecture. We in the class could watch things happen. We could watch jet engines grow from their elements to something like actual complexity. We could see equations being derived symbol by symbol. We could see families of curves fill a graph as physical conditions were changed. The lecture explained the characteristic curves, and the graphs of colored chalk showed how they were related to each other. We could see, and what we saw we remembered.

There was a special point, too, that required a visual aid more powerful than the chalkboard. This was a point easily forgotten, easily confused. It had to do with gas pressure waves in the tunnel of a jet. A subsonic wave might go down the tunnel with some care, "knowing where it was going, toward the light at the far end of the tunnel," and Professor Reynolds impersonated the wave, walking carefully across the room while peering ahead with his hands outstretched and emerging safely into the supposed light at the far end of the imaginary tunnel. But the supersonic pressure wave took no thought of where it was going, was unable, in fact, because of its speed to know what lay ahead—and here Professor Reynolds, having returned to his starting point, dashed madly across the room, seemingly heedless, almost frantic, with his hands appearing to cover his eyes; he brought up with a resounding crash against the opposite wall—and stepped back smiling.

"I'll never forget," Philip said afterward to Peter, "about that supersonic wave."

In the second twenty-minute drama, the seminar became a class in heat transfer. We were attending a lecture by Professor Reynolds that was nicely illustrated with colored slides and a display of some actual devices used in engineering practice. The projector had the latest arrangements for automatic operation and the pictures were excellent. Some were photographs of engineering apparatus using heat exchangers, some were charts or diagrams, and others were equations or formulas. A number of the slides showed chalkboard work by Professor Reynolds, which was now reproduced brilliantly in full color on the screen.

When the room was light again, Professor Reynolds showed and passed around the actual heat exchanger parts that he had brought. It was our role to pretend an interest in the engineering devices, but our real job was to see how the lecture was reinforced by this display of the actual things themselves.

This finished the second presentation, and we again became a seminar interested in teaching.

"Well?"

"Good," said James.

"Do you see any ways in which the slides are better than my drawing on the board?"

"Oh, yes," James replied, "they are bright and quick and clear."

"They are bright and clear," John observed, "if you have a strong bulb and a good screen."

"And," James continued, "the charts and graphs can be exactly accurate, which is more than you can hope for from drawings that you put on the board while you talk."

"Yes."

"Slides give a change of pace, too; a bit of novelty when you get tired of looking at the blackboard," suggested Bartholomew.

"That's right."

"The slides that show pictures of heat exchangers in real use and the actual pieces that you have here with you give a fellow a feeling that it's real," contributed Andrew.

"Yes, they do, don't they?" Professor Reynolds agreed. "Now do you see any disadvantages in using slides?"

"You can't watch a diagram grow on the screen as you do on the board, a line at a time," suggested Peter.

"Right."

"When you show slides you have to darken the room, at least partly," said Philip.

"Yes."

"Well," Philip was a bit embarrassed. "I'm apt to get sleepy."

"That's a very real point," admitted Professor Reynolds. "You can't see me, or at least not so well. I can't see you. Sometimes the ventilation isn't very good if the windows are shut, and—well, I lose my audience. It doesn't make the least bit of difference how fine the pictures are if the class's eyes are shut."

"You can't take notes in the dark, either," added Peter.

"Yes, that's another item."

"Well," said Professor Reynolds, "I have another show for you now. This is a movie show," and he started a moving picture projector buzzing for the third demonstration.

After suitable titles a bridge appeared on the screen, a bridge on a stormy day. It was a long steel suspension bridge, already reacting to a steady wind across it. The bridge was moving up and down. Even as we watched, the motion increased and the roadway along the bridge rose and fell in waves. A man on the bridge fled; a car was left to be whipped up and down as the rise and fall of the bridge became wilder. This was the famous film of the failure of the Tacoma Narrows bridge. We saw the bridge rise and fall with a period of several seconds, tip at a mad angle as one huge cable rose high, whip back as the other great cable rebounded. More and more wildly the great bridge leaped and rocked and swayed. Then a section gave way. From part of a span the roadway fell down into the black water below. For five minutes we watched the bridge and saw its destruction.

The film came in a cartridge that clipped onto the projector. The endless film strip rewound itself as it went, ready at once to be used again. Surely the ease and convenience of showing such a film were impressive.

The Tacoma Narrows film cartridge was unclipped, another cartridge clipped on, and we saw on the screen a greatly enlarged picture of oil flow in a bearing. Under certain conditions of speed and pressure the flow of oil became unstable; this was clear to us as we watched the motion of oil become erratic in the bearing. We saw this happen under a variety of conditions during the five minutes of the film.

Finally, and this in deference to the electrical engineers in our seminar, an electric arc appeared on the screen. The lower end of the arc was in a pool of mercury, and as mercury boiled from the heat of the electric current, the arc chamber was filled with low pressure mercury gas. The arc danced about over the surface of the mercury pool. Then a magnetic field was turned on, and the thin line of the arc ceased being fairly straight and became crooked, grotesque, bending into strange long paths until it was extinguished. This we saw also under various conditions of pressure and field strength, until our five minutes was up and the show was over.

"What do you think of it?" asked Professor Reynolds.

"Gosh, that's good," said Andrew. "I never saw anything like that bearing before. I didn't know it would look like that."

"I liked it," agreed Peter.

"You can see things happen," Andrew said.

"Things you couldn't see any other way," Peter added. "A movie can show something that only happens once, like the bridge, or you can slow things down, like the mercury arc, or speed them up if you want to."

"Better than television," Philip remarked.

"Yes, it often is," Professor Reynolds agreed. "And cheaper. Also," he pointed out, "if you want to see one section of the film over and over, you can. Or if you want to study a single moment of time, you can hold just one frame of the picture on the screen. But what," he asked, "are the disadvantages?"

"Well, the room has to be dark, even more than for slides," said Philip.

"And there's no variation," added Andrew. "If you want to see what it would look like if you changed the conditions just a bit—well, you can't."

"That's so, of course," said Professor Reynolds.

"They used to show us a lot of movies at Camembert College that were pretty foul," said Matthew. "They were sort of animated diagrams. They had one with a row of moving dots that was supposed to show how current traveled in a wire, and another that had waves wriggling out of a radar antenna."

"You didn't like the pretty pictures?" asked John.

"I did not."

"I've seen pictures like that, too," said Bartholomew. "Silly."

"Maybe they wanted to show you pictures of what you ought to know," John proposed.

"I could see such things better for myself," said Matthew.

"What could you see for yourself?" Philip asked.

"Oh, current in a wire, and waves, and things like that."

"Ah, movies inside your own head," suggested Philip.

"Every man his own movie show," urged John.

"Yes," said Peter, "but seriously, did the movies help you to visualize abstract things?"

"No," Matthew said flatly, "they didn't. What those movies showed I could see better inside my own head, as Philip puts it. You'd have to be pretty dumb to learn anything from them."

"Wait a minute," Peter interrupted. "Animated movies like that can sometimes be pretty well done. They aren't necessarily silly. But still, in spite of that, I wonder if it isn't usually better for you to see abstract things in your own head for yourself. That means visualizing, doesn't it?"

"Yes."

"Is there anything more important than learning to visualize?" asked Peter. There was no answer.

12

Doing is best

"Yes, that is a reason we often hear given for having laboratory work in the curriculum, but I wonder if it's really very true." Professor McWhorter had asked the seminar why laboratory work is included in a college course, and Thomas had suggested the platitude that laboratory work is to show that theory and experiment agree.

"At least," said Professor McWhorter, "I think there are a lot of better reasons for having the students work in laboratories. Really, you know, you don't have to convince the students that what the professor says is true; students are almost too ready to believe what's told them.

"And the theories from the lecture course don't *need* to be proved again by another student experiment, for they *have* been proved ever so many times already. So I'm afraid that wouldn't be a very good reason for having laboratory work in the curriculum. In fact, I can give you eight better reasons just offhand."

I had introduced Malcolm McWhorter as a professor who was exceptional in having given careful thought and planning to laboratory instruction, an aspect of the teaching business that most of us accept all too uncritically. Significantly, too, Dr. McWhorter was also vice-president of an electronics firm, the Vidar Corporation, and it might be guessed that he would sometimes look on present students as prospective employees.

"Indeed," he continued, "I think a rather better reason for laboratory work might be the other way around. Instead of the laboratory experiment proving that theory is almost true, perhaps the laboratory work is important because it shows that theory is not quite true.

"A theory or a model or an equation, whatever you want to call it, is always simplified from the actual facts of the real device. It is an idealization. Within certain limits a theory is nearly true, but outside those limits it often goes violently wrong. This is something students need to know.

"Let me list what I believe to be some of the reasons for laboratory work:

1. Shows the variations of results from theory.
2. Makes the subject more concrete.
3. Presents the same ideas at another time in another form.
4. Shows some relationships better than they can be shown by any other means.
5. Teaches techniques of measurement.
6. Suggests to the students how laboratory investigations are to be done.
7. Can teach how to prepare and present results.
8. Can ease the transition from paper and pencil to a working model, a great help to industry.

"I have talked about the first of these reasons already. The business of an analytical course is to make and use models. The business of the laboratory is to show where these models fail. Models are always incorrect if they are used in the wrong places.

"Second, the laboratory work makes the subject more concrete. A lot of the students have never had an opportunity to see what a megohm looks like. They soon find that a microfarad is a reasonable thing but a farad is not, however convenient it may be to talk about farads in lectures and use them in mathematics. A transistor is not a mark on a sheet of paper but a little box with some pins sticking out of the bottom that you put into a socket.

"I often think of one chap, a foreign student, who spent most of an afternoon trying to measure the characteristics of a transistor. He measured between one pair of terminals, and then another, and still another, and continued to get nothing. Everything he measured looked just like an open circuit. So finally he came around to see me and tell me he couldn't get any results. He was very much afraid he had ruined the transistor. I went to look, to see if I could tell what the trouble was, and I found out all right. He had a socket but there was no transistor in it, and he had spent the afternoon trying to measure the characteristics of an empty socket. Well, of course the trouble was that he didn't know what a transistor looked like.

"Third, it is one of the most important benefits of laboratory work that the student sees again the same ideas that were given in the lecture course. This is planned repetition of a most valuable kind, for the point of view is quite different in the laboratory. The student doesn't feel it to be tiresome, but nevertheless he has to bring again to the front of his mind the relationships with which he is dealing. When this is done after the short delay that laboratory schedules usually provide, it gives just the right kind of repetition for good learning, the kind in which principles already known are used again in a form that is similar but not identical.

"Perhaps this would be a good place to mention the perennial difficulty of scheduling. Some teachers like to have laboratory work scheduled to synchronize with a lecture course so that a lecture on theory is accompanied immediately by a related experiment. This cannot ordinarily be done, partly because of the practical difficulties of scheduling with a finite amount of equipment and partly because students are not always prepared to do at once in the laboratory all that they hear about in lectures.

"A few teachers would like to have experimental work in the laboratory actually precede the theory that tells what it is all about, so that hopefully the students can discover some new ideas for themselves. This idealistic aim is ordinarily impractical because discovering new ideas takes an unconscionable amount of time. Anyway, if the students don't know what the experimental work is all about, the logic of what they are doing is apt to be foggy both then and always.

"Other teachers like to have the laboratory course come a good bit later than the theory. This gives the advantage of planned repetition, and also it lets you arrange the laboratory course so that a student can learn the necessary techniques before he has to use them in an experiment. Another advantage is that a given experiment can be related to any or all of the course on theory rather than being tied to one specific subject.

"I suspect you may have gathered from my remarks that I believe that the most practical arrangement is to have the laboratory work follow the lectures on theory after some convenient interval, but I do not want to insist on this as a necessity. What I do want to urge very strongly is that a laboratory course should be *self-standing* and not leaning for any necessary support on another course.

"Fourth, it is often easier to show the effect of some change—let us say a change of frequency—by watching the output wave form on an oscilloscope than it is to work out the same effect from the equations or the theory. When an amplifier, for instance, has been put together in a laboratory, you can then feed in a sine wave signal of constant amplitude and see what happens to the amplifier output as you turn the frequency knob on the input signal generator. There are dozens of such situations where laboratory results are more graphic and therefore more educational than mathematical solutions.

"Another good feature of laboratory work is that you can often see how precise an element must be in actual fact. Perhaps the book says that a resistor should have forty-eight thousand ohms resistance, but the resistor that you have in the bin has fifty thousand. Is this all right? Well, usually it is but sometimes it isn't, and it's really important to know. It's important, too, that the nominal value of a resistor or a capacitor or some other element is not always its actual value. This whole subject of tolerance makes a big difference in practical design work.

"Fifth, there is the very obvious fact that laboratory work teaches techniques of measurement. The boys learn about measuring instruments, and what can be done and what can't—the present state of the art. For instance, it is easy to measure time to one part in 10^8, but the same precision in measuring capacitance is impossible.

"They learn about errors and the sources of errors, of systematic errors and random errors. They find that the measuring process itself produces an error in the measured quantity. They see that there is always random error in reading an instrument, and there may be other instrumental errors, too.

"A predictable student aberration comes when a boy gets hold of an ammeter or a voltmeter or some other instrument that is seriously wrong. Maybe it has been dropped on the floor, or is partially burned out, or has had some other sad accident. The student tries to use this damaged instrument with little success, and it seems to make such an impression on his previously simple faith that for months thereafter he blames any error on a damaged meter.

"Then there is another time in the career of students when they want to blame everything that seems wrong on the error of idealization. This is when they first find that theories and models and equations may be inexact, and that assumptions may not be in complete agreement with fact. Then the boys say that inexact theory is the reason for anything they don't like, even though it may be perfectly evident that the real source of error is a loose connection. This is a stage of student development that lasts for several months, and then they get over it. They get over it when they learn that measurements are made to find out something.

"This leads to my sixth point, which is that laboratory work, even with set experiments, can give the student an idea that it is really possible to learn new things by experimental work. New ideas and contributions to knowledge come from observations and measurements of what actually happens and not from reading books. Of course, one man may produce a new theory based on what another man has observed, but the purpose of the theory is to fit the observations.

"Maybe the student wants to go on in his academic life to some future research for a thesis or dissertation. The first step is for him to see the part that experiment must play. This is a view or an attitude that is encouraged by leaving part of the laboratory course work optional and undefined. If the student has to decide what he wants to do and how, and what measurements to make, and what instruments to use, he will be the better for it—even though it may come to little. It is hardly to be expected that he will really find anything new in his early investigations although perhaps later on—who knows?

"Seventh, there are reports. There is nothing so controversial about laboratories as the way to write reports. At one extreme, instrument readings are recorded in a notebook, and computations, together with an extremely brief account of work done, are written in the notebook by the student before he leaves the laboratory. The book is not to be taken away from the laboratory.

"At the other extreme, each laboratory report is written in ink or typed; curves are drawn with instruments; the several sheets from introduction to conclusions and an appended data sheet, including a list of serial numbers of all instruments, are neatly fastened into a manila folder for submission a week after the experiment is done.

"The book that never leaves the lab gives no opportunity to think about the work. The inked and drafted report absorbs a good many hours of student time. Some teachers say that the laboratory notebook is more like real life in an industrial laboratory; other teachers say that formal reports have to be written in real life, and a student should know how. The only reasonable conclusion is that both are right and both are wrong, and the least unsatisfactory decision is some sort of compromise.

"In fact, I like to use laboratory notebooks with permanent binding and numbered pages, which the students can take home with them for computations and a brief write-up for most of the experiments, and then require a longer and more formal report (though not with curves and diagrams in India ink) on one or two experiments a term. Good English, clear writing, and correct grammar are expected in all reports, and even the shortest ones must make sense to a reader who doesn't know what it is all about. This seems to me to be a good compromise, but perhaps someone else thinks differently.

"Now, finally, to offer an eighth value of laboratory work, I change hats and speak as an employer of young engineers. Laboratory experience can do a lot to ease the transition of a young man from paper and pencils to working models. Far be it from me to suggest that industry does not consume paper and pencils, for which our little company has to pay a big bill, but the final outcome of engineering in industry is usually something that works—an item of equipment or a device or a system. My company might make an amplifier; another company might make a spectrometer, a pH meter, a rocket control system, a telescope, or a laser.

"Of course I don't expect that a boy in school is going to learn to design an actual commercial laser or an amplifier or a pH meter, but he can find out a lot about real life in a very short time by handling real things in laboratories. This will make life easier for him when he gets a job, besides easing the strain on the company that takes him in. I appeal to you as future teachers to give your boys this advantage.

"There," said Professor McWhorter, "those add up to eight reasons for laboratory work that are better, I think, than proving that the professor is always right. Now, how can these things be done?

"In my opinion, the only absolutely one-hundred-percent necessary thing in a laboratory course is a good instructor. He should certainly take a maximum of interest, but probably give a minimum of directions. He must want to give lots of help, but not do all the planning. It doesn't make a great deal of difference what the experiments are about or what you do or don't do. You can't do everything. And you don't learn all the basic laws in the laboratory anyway.

"It is extremely important that the value of a laboratory does not lie in doing what you say you are doing but in all the incidents of reality and measurement that go with it. A laboratory is not to teach specifics but by-products. Do you agree?"

"Yes," said Peter, "I think I do."

Philip looked worried. "I had always sort of thought . . . I don't know just how to put it . . . that the laws . . . well, that the laws were *right* . . .

things like Newton's laws, and Coulomb's, and Maxwell's. But now that you say so, and I really think about it, I suppose they do all come from experimental results. I mean, I suppose, at least when they were first devised, that they might have been a little wrong."

"No." Matthew was firm. "Laws like these are laws of nature. Newton didn't make the law, he only discovered it."

"Oh, golly," moaned Andrew.

"I would point out," said Professor McWhorter, "that Maxwell proposed one of his laws as just a guess. We still call it Maxwell's hypothesis. And Maxwell himself treated Coulomb's famous inverse-square law of electric attraction as merely a good approximation; he showed that if the exponent of the distance-squared term was not exactly 2 it was at least quite close, for experiment showed it to be between 1.99 and 2.01 or something like that. Maxwell certainly didn't consider that Coulomb's law, or his own, or probably even Newton's, was divinely inspired. Maybe one of the reasons that we have tended to talk about models instead of laws in recent years is that it helps remove the halo."

"I am not just sure, sir," Bartholomew said, "that I know what a model is."

"Well, I think a model is an idealization of an actual fact. A model of a transistor, for instance, is a circuit that works in a certain way—very like a real transistor but simpler. Maybe it's a physical model, and you could put it in a circuit (if such a thing as the model could really exist) instead of the transistor, in which case it isn't much different from what we used to call an equivalent circuit. Or perhaps it's a mathematical model, which means that it's an equation to tell how the thing works."

"There was an article in a magazine not long ago," remarked Peter.

"On models?"

"Yes." Peter turned to me. "Shall I bring it around next time, sir?"

"Yes," I replied, "please do. Better still, why don't you just tell us next time what the article is all about?"

Peter looked a bit taken aback but he said, gamely, "Very well, sir. I'll try."

13
Models

"It's called *An Operational View*," said Peter at the next meeting, "and I don't know what that means, but the article begins right away about models.* A mathematical model is an equation, it says, and a conceptual model can be just an idea in somebody's mind. You can make a plaster model of a mountain and call it a relief map. The general idea is that any model keeps the essential features of the original but ignores the details.

"Our minds are just full of models, it says, and the article calls them mental models. You have in your mind a mental model of this table here, and that's all that you have in your mind, because of course you don't have the table in your mind but only your mental model of it. And you have some kind of a mental model of this building, for instance, and you have a mental model of an electron, and you have one of the solar system.

"Well, the article says that you believe some of these models a lot more than you believe others. In fact, that seems to be the whole idea of the article—that you have a lot of faith in your mental model of this table or this building, but you probably don't have nearly as much faith in your mental model of something like the inside of a molecule.

"According to the article, a mental model is dependable if you can predict from it. For instance, my mental model of this building tells me that just outside that door there's a drinking fountain; all right, I go

*American Scientist, Vol. 52, No. 4, p. 388A, 1964.

outside that door and sure enough there really is a drinking fountain there, so my mental model was a good one.

"On the other hand, my mental model of Washington, D.C., tells me that the White House is on Massachusetts Avenue at F Street, but when I am in Washington and go to Massachusetts Avenue at F Street there isn't any White House there at all, but only the Union Station—well, my mental model was wrong."

"I don't have to *think* there's a drinking fountain just outside that door; I *know* there is," said Matthew.

"Just a high degree of probability," said Peter. "You *could* be wrong."

"I could *not* be wrong," Matthew insisted. "I saw it there."

"Perhaps it was a hallucination," suggested Peter, "or maybe you dreamed it, or it could all have been done with mirrors. There are all kinds of possibilities. Tell me,"—Peter lowered his voice confidentially—"do you often see things that aren't there?"

"Why you big monkey!" Matthew was really annoyed. "I don't ever see things that aren't there!"

"Don't you, really? Well, that's good. That makes the probability of that drinking fountain's being there really pretty high."

"It's a certainty," the goaded Matthew glared.

"Well, when you say 'certainty', what you mean is that the probability is really quite high. So says my article. And," Peter added, forestalling another explosion from Matthew, "you will recognize that no certainty can be absolute, since even your best mental models are made on the strength of only a finite number of observations.

"Take Newton's law of acceleration, for instance. It was thought to be Right with a capital R until people began talking about relativity. But sometimes, with more data, our mental models have to be patched up a bit—or even changed completely."

" 'Doubt thou the stars are fire,' " quoted Thomas unexpectedly, " 'Doubt that the sun doth move. . . . ' "

"Well, yes. These do seem to be mental models that have been doubted by scientists in recent years, don't they?"

"How do I know that *you* are real, Peter, and not a nightmare?" asked Andrew sweetly. "Maybe I ate something that didn't agree with me, and you are the result. A bit of mustard. . . . " Perhaps Andrew was also a reader of the classics.

"You don't, of course," Peter agreed. "And to me, you are merely a concept, my mental model. But I shall hope you are real."

"That's good of you," said Andrew.

"This same idea of probability is familiar enough when we are talking about scientific theories." Peter was serious again. "What is the probability of an expanding universe being a good mental model, as suggested by observations of the red shift? Maybe you feel it's a high probability; maybe you think it's a low one. And what do I mean by *good*? I mean, will it predict correctly. Can you use your mental model to tell you what to expect at some future time? For instance, will Newton's law tell me what will happen tomorrow?"

"Newton's law will be all right if you don't go too fast," suggested Philip.

"Yes, that's about it," Peter agreed. "My article says that even the best models have limits beyond which they do not apply. That's why it's just a waste of time to try to speculate beyond the limits of your data. You simply can't think about what happened before time began or what there is beyond all space, because even space and time are mental models and they have uncertain limits. So just don't worry."

"These," said John, "are not subjects that keep me awake nights."

"No," agreed James, "they wouldn't."

"It seems to follow," Peter went on, "that there is really no way to be sure about the reality of anything. Some people like to think that a good mental model is similar to physical reality, and the closer the model comes to fitting the data, the nearer it is to reality. But this, my article says, is merely faith. You can believe in a physical reality if you like, and it does seem to be a useful hypothesis for making predictions that turn out well, but just remember that it remains a matter of faith and that you believe it because it is useful to do so.

"And what all this leads to," Peter concluded, "is that our mental models are good *if* they are useful but not otherwise."

"Well," said James, "I shouldn't have thought that *faith* was just the word. To me, faith means believing in something . . . in something that it is good to believe in."

"Yes," Peter replied, "I guess that's right. Isn't that just what I have been saying? It's what I meant to say. I believe quite a lot in tables and chairs and more or less in atoms and electrons, and maybe I believe in things hoped for and things not seen, and one kind of belief just seems to merge into another. Nothing is infinitely true, not even tables and chairs, but all the things we think we know are more or less probable. Every mental model has its probability price tag. So says my article.

"And that," said Peter, "is that."

"Thank you," I said to Peter, and to the seminar, "What do you think of it?"

"Well," remarked Philip after a moment, "maybe so. Or maybe not. I haven't thought it through yet. But supposing there is really something in this article, Peter, what does it have to do with teaching? Anything?"

"Are you asking me?"

"Yes. What do you think?"

"It seems to me that it has a lot to do with teaching," Peter replied. "What it means to me is that I must not teach anything to a class as if it were certain and final. All I know, and all that anybody knows, is that a law is useful within limits."

"Within limits?"

"Yes. Limits of time and space and so on. Newton's laws are just about right at low speeds. Hooke's law of strain is pretty good if you don't have too much stress. Maxwell's equations are fine now, I guess, but who knows what the situation was ten million years ago? Maybe electromagnetic radiation was different then."

"Light from the distant stars, . . . " suggested Philip.

"Well?"

"Yes, I see. The red shift."

"Exactly. So that's the way it goes. Everything we know is within some kind of limits, and I ought not to teach that anything is true everywhere and forever."

"It seems to me that there's something else, too," suggested Philip.

"What?"

"Well, that experiments come first and laws come second. A law or a model or an equation is a generalization of observations, isn't it?"

"Yes."

"Then I mustn't teach that 'this is the law, and just look at all these observed facts that result from it.' What I ought to say is, 'here are all the facts we have observed, and this is the law we have devised to describe them.' "

"I guess that's right," said Peter.

14

Know thyself

These words of the Delphic Oracle were Professor Harman's text. I had introduced him as a leader, a teacher with a most devoted following, a seeker who in turn was sought.

"Through many centuries, and intensively in the last few, we have developed knowledge," he said, "and now we don't know exactly what to do with it.

"Some knowledge is technical and professional. Some is general and social. Some is self-knowledge, knowledge of one's self.

"The term self-knowledge is an open-ended one, and to attempt to define it precisely would be to limit its scope. But self-knowledge would surely imply progress toward some such goals as these:

"Release from the grip of outdated emotional responses, from patterns of fear or hostility that at one time had protective value but are not appropriate in current situations.

"Clarification of the bases of one's beliefs, prejudices, and values; movement away from allegiance to unconsciously determined beliefs and values and toward commitment to consciously chosen ones. . . . ''

Professor Harman read these two paragraphs from a page that he had passed out to the seminar. "These are not all the implications of self-knowledge," he said, "but they are enough to talk about this afternoon.

"The basic question for a teacher seems to me to be this: among the three kinds of knowledge—technical knowledge, general knowledge, and self-knowledge—what is there that can be taught?

"Let me suggest that we teachers can work toward several ends which are as follows:

1. A teacher can impart knowledge.
2. We can help students meet new situations as they arise, almost from day to day.
3. We must try to prepare students to make the long-term decisions of the next generation. This will require maturity, independence, creativity, and judgment.
4. We may perhaps help the student to study himself and to consider the source of his own value systems.
5. We can hope to produce motivation or to change existing motivation.

"Here are five goals of teaching. You will see that all but the first of these goals might be called noninformational."

Professor Harman's ideas brought some special excitement to James and, it seemed, to some of the other young men of the seminar. James was alert to every word, responsive as a tuned instrument.

"Do you propose," he ventured, "that the purpose of teaching should be to change behavior rather than to give facts?"

"No," replied Professor Harman. "That would seem to me to be inappropriate. I do not mean to propose any tremendous revolution, but there *are* more extreme views. Carl Rogers, who was a clinical psychologist as well as a professor, went far beyond my proposal in making these astonishing remarks:

> It seems to me that anything that can be taught to another is relatively inconsequential, and has little or no significant influence on behavior. That sounds so ridiculous I can't help but question it at the same time I present it.
>
> I realize increasingly that I am only interested in learning which significantly influences behavior. Quite possibly this is simply a personal idiosyncrasy.
>
> I have come to feel that the only learning which significantly influences behavior is self-discovered, self-appropriated learning.
>
> I find it very rewarding to learn, in groups, in relationships with one person as in therapy or by myself.

"Well, Carl Rogers certainly dropped a bomb, and no doubt that was what he meant to do." Professor Harman paused, waiting for the seminar to consider Carl Rogers' iconoclasm and, hopefully, to comment. Philip was the first to find words.

"Does Carl Rogers mean that all our classes are a waste of time?"

Professor Harman looked around, inviting a response from the seminar, and presently Peter replied.

"No-o. I don't think he means exactly that. He just considers classwork inconsequential. Do partial differential equations significantly influence your behavior?"

"Influence my behavior? Why, yes. I expect they'll have something to do with my getting a job."

"That would be quite insignificant, I expect, to a clinical psychologist," said Peter.

"Carl Rogers is thinking of something deeper within you," suggested James.

Professor Harman then drew three circles on the blackboard.

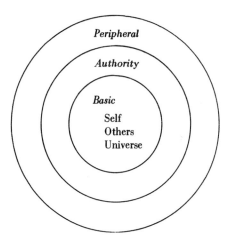

Peripheral

Authority

Basic

Self
Others
Universe

"Milton Rokeach has drawn a diagram of what he calls *belief systems*, and here is the essential part of it. Our *basic* beliefs are deep within us. It is hard to change basic beliefs because they are so tied to emotions. They are formed quite early in life, probably adopted from our parents, and before we ever start to school.

"Beliefs based on *authority* we usually accept without much question. Authority can be the mother, the church, the Bible, the library, or all of these. Beliefs based on authority are reached at a fairly early age, and they can be changed only with difficulty.

"What we ordinarily call our 'beliefs' are the *peripheral* ones. These result from education, and these, it seems, *can* be changed by what we learn in school or otherwise.

"Of course it is valuable and important to have good peripheral beliefs, and it is in this circle that the contribution of the schools is most evident. It is not evident that anything taught in the schools can change either of the two inner circles.

"I suspect that it was these inner circles that Carl Rogers was concerned with. The basic belief systems are exceedingly hard to alter. It certainly cannot be done by any classroom teaching, and if you are mainly concerned with basic beliefs you will understand his emphasis on learning in small groups or even alone.

"I think it is in this light that we should view Rogers' statement that 'My experience has been that I cannot teach another person how to teach.' "

"Can a college teacher do anything at all with these inner circles—to improve them, I mean?" asked Peter.

"Yes, I think so. What you *are* carries over to the students in what you say and in every decision that you make concerning them. In any discussion that goes deeper than the peripheral level, the give and take between you and the students will help them establish a system of values. We must not avoid discussion of basic problems if we are to help a student in his basic beliefs. Carl Rogers says that a teacher must drop his own defensiveness, for a highly defensive teacher will encourage exchange on the intellectual level only, and no individual feelings will come out, and then the discussion will be of peripheral values only.

"Everyone has his own system of values. Some things you value more than others and some less. For instance, since you are in this seminar on teaching, you probably value intellectual attainments fairly highly. The value that you place on the possession of money is probably less, and on the display of wealth still less. In this way you have constructed for yourself a set of values of all things, from honor or love at one end to—well, to something pretty ordinary at the other."

" 'I could not love thee, dear, so much,' " murmured John, " 'loved I not honor more.' "

"Exactly. And what can we do to help a student build up a suitable scale of values? Well, values are usually learned by emulation. Particularly, a student tends to identify, as the psychologists say, with someone he admires. Does this offer a suggestion for us?

"Unfortunately perhaps, studies show that changes of value systems by students in college are likely to be slight, very slight indeed, and hardly noticeable above the 'noise'. Still, we can hope to reinforce the good values, and perhaps with some people, to bring order into disordered thinking.

"If a man is struggling with a value system that is really badly mixed up he is close to having what the psychologist would term a neurosis. Some of these near-neurotic people are familiar types. There is the self-effacing type who is full of fears. There is the resigned type who expects the worst and for whom life has no meaning. There is the perfectionist who is never satisfied, particularly with himself. There is the arrogant-vindictive type who believes the world is hostile to him personally; typically he has headaches and other pains. And there is the narcissistic type who overrates and admires himself and resents routine.

"Fortunately, very few people are so badly off in their value systems that a psychiatrist is needed, but perhaps we can say that a good many people lean a little in one or another of these neurotic directions. At least, everyone can find a way, if he wants to, of not reaching his full potential. It might be that we could help him find his balance.

"Finally I would like to suggest two thoughts that I believe to be important. First, it seems to me that the predominant objective of education is to help each student to realize his full potential. This is quite different, you see, from the objective of making him a useful citizen. And second, I am rather afraid that our whole society is lacking in vision and our situation is precarious. Our basic beliefs and values have not advanced with our mentalities. Emotions that were fitted to survival in the Stone Age are dangerous in a man with a nuclear intellect."

It was clear from what Professor Harman had told us that he preferred discussion to a lecture. He preferred asking questions to answering, awaiting comment to speaking, and he wanted the young men of the seminar to seek answers to questions that they themselves raised.

The men felt challenged and perhaps even inspired, and discussion continued at some length and with spirit. It may be that the contributions by the seminar were not particularly great nor perhaps even new, but the benefit of what each young man said was to himself.

"Values," said Philip. "A set of values. Yes, I suppose I have one. I don't know that I know just what it is, though."

"I suppose we do have them," Peter considered, "but I couldn't write mine down."

"We'd rate things like truth and loyalty fairly high, I expect, and a good dinner or a warm overcoat somewhat lower."

"Depends on the weather," grunted John.

"Shut up," said Philip dispassionately. "What I mean to say is, your scale of values, Peter, and mine, and even John's here, must be rather alike."

"Yes, but other people's mightn't be, do you think? Take a communist Chinese from a Sinkiang village or a Hottentot from a hut in Bantustan, wouldn't theirs be different?"

"From yours and mine? Yes, I'm sure they would. Even, I suppose, different from John's, although that's hard to say."

"G-r-r-r," said John.

"Well," remarked Peter, "that reminds me of what a chap in the American Embassy said when I was in London on a Fulbright fellowship. He said, 'The English have different words for things that don't much matter, such as spanner or biscuit or the bonnet of a car, but when they speak of honor or truth or law, they mean exactly what we do—and that's what counts.' "

"The same scale of values?"

"Yes," said Peter.

"And that's why we get along with them pretty well?"

"Yes."

"And maybe we'd get along pretty well with anybody who had the same scale of values we have?"

"I expect we would."

"But we might have trouble getting along with someone who had quite a different scale of values?"

"I suppose we might."

"I suppose we might at that," said Philip. "In fact—we do. We do, don't we?"

"Yes," said Peter, "we do."

15

Saltation

"It is a pleasure," I said, "to introduce Professor W. H. Cowley. I am sure you all know Professor Cowley as our authority on American higher education and comparative higher education. You may not also know that he was formerly president of Hamilton College and that he speaks from administrative as well as teaching experience. I know, and I expect many of you know, that Professor Cowley's unique insight into the history of universities helps us to understand the peculiar thing we are today.

"A mathematician does not feel that he is well acquainted with a function if he knows that function for only one value of time, but if he knows how the function behaved through all earlier times, he not only feels quite well acquainted with the present, but he can even look into the future.

"Ah, yes; Taylor's theorem," and though I was enjoying my own flight of fancy I returned to business. "So I present to you Professor Cowley who will speak on *The Environment of the College Teacher*."

Dr. Cowley looked benevolently at the seminar, "This discussion evolves from the assumption that the environment largely controls what a college teacher may and may not do. In general, college teachers give little thought to these environmental limitations and compulsions, but they do consistently influence teaching.

"To comprehend the current instructional complex, a look at the situation of a century ago will help. The colleges then had only one method of instruction, the recitation method, which was not a teaching method at all but primarily an examination method. The teacher sought only to discover whether the student had studied his lessons. Much drill resulted, of course, but no real teaching.

"Still farther back, the year 1776 was marked by at least six great events:

1. Watt's steam engine ended the age of muscle power and began the age of machine power.
2. Adam Smith's book, 'The Wealth of Nations,' was published. This was one of the greatest books of all history. It provided the economic theory for developing the steam engine and all the other power machines that followed.
3. This year was central to the period 1774–1778 in which Lavoisier's study of chemistry, including his law of combustion, broke the bottleneck that had been holding back all science.
4. The Declaration of Independence stated in Jefferson's words that the power to govern derives from the consent of the governed.
5. The separation of church and state, also furthered by Jefferson, led to taking education out of the hands of organized religion where it had been lodged for centuries.
6. The outlawing of the inherited privileges involved in primogeniture led to the broadening of the base of education.

"The first three of these, which I have come to call the *Power Saltation*, increased the power of man over the forces of nature. The other three spread this power throughout society.

"An immediate result of the power saltation was the expansion of knowledge into areas that would now be called science and engineering. Indeed, the United States Military Academy, which was opened at West Point in 1802, was primarily an engineering school, and West Point produced most American engineers in all fields during the first half of the nineteenth century.

"Originally a 'civil engineer' was one who was not a military engineer, and the Rensselaer Polytechnic Institute opened at Troy, New York, in 1824, to offer instruction in applied scientific subjects to civilians. In these early years America followed the continental European plan of giving applied scientific subjects in separate schools, sometimes called polytechnic institutes or institutes of technology as the German counterpart is the *technische Hochschule*.

"*The Land-Grant College Act of 1862* changed this situation in America and brought science and engineering into the evolving American university. This was possible in the new America, although it was not at that time acceptable in European universities because of their traditional emphasis on literary subjects; their abhorrence of those engaged in physical labor; and their disdain of those involved in commerce or, as they called it in Britain, 'trade'.

"With the growth of knowledge, education, which had previously been mainly literary, became broader. Whether in universities or in *technische Hochschulen*, learning expanded into many new subjects; and since no one could be expected to be in command of them all, specialization became a central fact of the modern world.

"The result of the expansion of learning, the reorientation of education, and the reorganization of universities and colleges was the vast *Education Saltation*, which reached an unprecedented height between 1861 and 1876 and has continued ever since. In this great expansion we borrowed many developments from Germany where two hundred and seven specialized schools, unconnected with universities, were already teaching agriculture, engineering, forestry, navigation, and teacher training. Our imports from Germany included the lecture system, laboratories, seminars, clinical teaching, and the elective principle of studies. Even the blackboard came to us, it appears, from Germany.

"English education, which had given us our earlier pattern, was designed to lead to the Master's degree; the PhD was a German import that became popular in this country because so many of our best university men went to Germany for advanced study during this period.

"The elective principle took hold in America toward the end of the nineteenth century, too. Before this time a student in a university did not specialize, for it was not too much to hope that an educated man would be well versed in all lines of general knowledge. But specialization began with the *Great Saltation* and continued until it led President Lowell to speak slightingly of a Harvard dissertation that had as its subject 'the left hind leg of the paleozoic cockroach.'

"There were then, and there are now, lots of criticisms of specialization, but specialists keep right on specializing, adding new specialties, and training new specialists. *It cannot be otherwise.* The growth of knowledge continues unremittingly with high profit to the race, and we cannot stop specializing. Nor does any intelligent person want to. Instead, the best informed critics of specialization realize that they must now turn their attention not to the elimination of specialization but to maintaining the proper relationship between specialized education and general education."

Professor Cowley stopped for an instant and turned a page of his outline.

"Now let us leave the past and look to the present. Let us agree that modern education has two aspects: (1) special education for one's special functions in society, for one's work or profession, and (2) general education for one's responsibilities as a parent and as a citizen.

"In some subjects a *compartmental plan* is used, with general education in certain college years followed by specialized education in later years, possibly postgraduate. This plan has long been in effect in medicine, theology, and law, but rarely in science or engineering.

"The *concurrent plan* is almost universal in the latter, with some time devoted to general education and some to specialized education in each of the undergraduate years."

This remark brought the first interruption of the afternoon. Peter asked, "Sir, how can you tell special education from general education? That is, if an engineering student takes a course in geology, is it special or general?"

"That's a good question," replied Professor Cowley, "and it arises very often. Does a student of chemistry, for example, take a course in English to prepare for his special function as a chemist or for his general responsibility as a citizen? Why does a student of psychology take a course in calculus? When a medical student takes a biology course in his undergraduate years, might he not seem already to have started his special professional education? I think the medical student would probably call biology a medical subject."

"Isn't a biology course for a man who is going to study medicine different from a biology course taught for somebody else?" asked Peter.

"It can be, but I like to divide courses into three types—democentric, practicentric, and logocentric.

"*Democentric* courses are for everybody, for a general knowledge of the subject. *Practicentric* courses are organized to train practitioners. *Logocentric* courses teach fundamental theory and are primarily designed for those interested in 'extending the boundaries of knowledge' of the subject.

"To return to your question, a course in biology may be democentric, that is, for everybody, but it is more commonly organized from a practicentric point of view. Do I make this clear?"

"Yes," said Peter, "Thank you." And Andrew added, "Sir, it depends on what the prof is shooting at, doesn't it?"

"The aim of the professor? Well, I'd express it a little differently," explained Professor Cowley. "It is essentially its organization that determines the nature of a course, but the professor's 'aim' determines his method of organizing his material.

"There are three *aims* that professors basically have in their teaching. One aim is to teach *know-about*. Another is to teach *know-how*. The third is to impart *attitudes* or can I say 'know-what'? Both know-about and know-how are obviously important, but perhaps acquiring attitudes is most important of all.

"There are two approaches to attitudes, the direct and the indirect. The direct approach can mean, for example, requiring high standards of work and thus bringing the student to acceptance if not approval of high standards. Unfortunately, the direct approach does not work for imparting other kinds of attitudes, because simply telling a student how he ought to feel about something borders on preaching, and that he dislikes and hence refuses to heed.

"But the indirect approach is happening continually. In Emerson's words, 'What you are speaks a thousand times more eloquently than what you say.' Instructors cannot help but teach attitudes—some good, some bad.

"It is very, very difficult for any person to know the attitudes that he instills in his students by his example, because these are so much a part of himself. However, an attempt to state his aims clearly to himself may lead to a thorough overhauling of his teaching methods.

"I must say again that the importance of attitudes cannot be overstressed. Attitudes dominate the psychological environment. Consider, for instance, the disdain of labor, a Greek attitude coming down to the present, and the resulting disdain of practicentric knowledge, which is seen in the conflict between so-called material and spiritual development. This has influenced the growth of universities in many regions of the world, and even today a great part of higher education is still literary.

"Now, how are these three aims to be achieved? In all subjects, *verbal* methods of education are of central importance, and verbal skill is required in presentation. Rhetorical skill and mastery of vocal equipment are therefore necessary, as well as ability in writing. Thus words are the stock-in-trade of all teachers—perhaps most crucially in literary subjects but very significantly in teaching of every kind.

"I shall conclude then," said Dr. Cowley, "by explaining why I have not told you what you want to know. Everybody wants to know 'how to do it.' You hoped I would tell you 'how to teach.' What is the right teaching method? But indeed there *is* no right teaching method. It would be indefensible to talk about teaching methods without showing how they are related to the many associated variables.

"I should like to list ten such variables, ten independent variables, each of which can have many values:

1. The subject
2. The content of the subject chosen for instruction
3. The students
4. The teacher
5. The teacher's purpose or aim
6. The organization of the material
7. The method of presentation
8. Out-of-class work by students
9. Examinations
10. General curricular structure

I have mentioned a few of these ten variables: the subject—scientific or literary; the purpose or aim—know-about, know-how, or attitudes; the organization of the material—whether democentric, practicentric, or logocentric; and the method of presentation, which is primarily verbal, whether by lecture or textbook or demonstration. Others of these ten variables I have not mentioned, such as examinations, out-of-class work, the great variety of our students, and the different personalities of teachers.

"The combinations of these variables are infinite, and thus teaching takes an infinite variety of forms. No method of teaching applies in every situation, and no man can teach in every situation, no matter how well prepared he may be."

16

Andrew on women

The bell rang in Room 308.

"A week ago we heard from Professor Cowley," I said.

"Yes, and he left his talk with us, too, all written out," added Andrew.

"Professor Cowley is very good about providing a copy of his talks."

"Sir," asked Philip, "about attitudes. What did he mean about not using direct methods?"

I passed the question on, as teachers like to do. "Peter, what is an example of the direct method?"

"Well, I suppose if you tell a class, 'do this,' or 'don't do that,' you are using a direct method. If you say, 'do be honest in examinations,' or 'don't come to class in a dirty shirt,' it sounds too much like preaching, and the students won't pay much attention."

"And the indirect method?"

"Perhaps if the teacher himself is always clean and neat this will be noticed and the class will follow his lead even if he doesn't say anything."

"Like," suggested John, "the teacher always has a nice short haircut." James, who wore rather a thatch, colored a little but said nothing.

"However, the teacher can insist on neat homework papers," I added, "papers that are clear and logical, expressed in correct English, perhaps even with what the mathematician calls elegance—this I think is the direct method. I believe Professor Cowley said the direct method could be really effective for this one purpose only; that is, for maintaining high standards of work."

"It seems to me," said James (this was his usual gambit), "that the university has no business trying to dictate things like personal appearance."

"Like washing behind the ears, for instance?" suggested John, grinning.

"Oh, shut up," snapped James.

"Well, but seriously," Peter remarked, "you get all kinds of boys from high school. Some of them don't know any better."

"Any better than what?" asked Philip.

"Any better than to be dirty and messy. Isn't that something that Professor Cowley would call an attitude?"

"I think," said James, "that Professor Cowley meant something higher than washing when he spoke of attitudes."

" 'Cleanliness is next to godliness,' " quoted John, "but what kind of thing do you mean?"

"Oh," suggested James, a little vaguely, "professional ethics for instance."

"When I had a job with Edam Electronics," stated Andrew, "their idea of professional ethics was don't be screwy."

"Well," Peter took it upon himself to close the discussion, "maybe attitudes are ethics, and maybe attitudes are washing, and maybe attitudes are both, but you know as well as I do that Professor Cowley is perfectly right. You can't preach about attitudes, but you can set a good example. And *I* think that this is about half of the teacher's job."

"Well. . . . " said James.

"And so do I," added Andrew. "We all have to get jobs, and you can't get a job if you look like a . . . "

"Keep it clean," warned John.

". . . like something the cat dragged in, I was going to say."

"*Must* we put it on a basis of getting a job?" protested James.

"No," said Andrew, "you can put it on the basis of learning to act like a gentleman, if you think that's better. Math and physics aren't all a freshman needs to learn."

"Golly," moaned Philip. "This from you?"

"Well, and why not?" Andrew was belligerent. Perhaps he felt embarrassed at being drawn in defense of his code, so I provoked Peter on another subject.

"Peter, did you say you thought general education a waste of time?"

"No, I don't think so, sir. No, I don't think I said that. It seems to me that everybody needs English and economics and some history. . . . "

"Hey, wait," Philip interrupted. "English and econ aren't 'general' subjects. They're 'tool' subjects. You need them in your business."

"Possibly 'democentric' or possibly 'practecentric,' depending on how they are organized," I suggested. " Suppose the English course is on poetry and drama."

"Oh, good," said James.

John groaned audibly.

"Well, what's the matter with you?" Philip asked him.

"I don't think I'll do my doctor's thesis in poetry."

"I'd just like to see my boss at Edam Electronics when I hand him my week's report in verse," sighed Andrew.

"Let's make English practical," suggested John sweetly. "Then maybe James could learn to spell."

"Oaf," said James.

"Andrew seems to favor a good deal of specialization," I remarked, hoping to bring the discussion back to Professor Cowley's ideas again.

"You've got to specialize," insisted Andrew. "Everybody specializes more and more all the time. Why, I'll bet a solid-state guy like Thomas here doesn't even know how to start an electric motor."

"I do," said Thomas, "But I doubt if you know much about the Fermi level in a semiconductor."

"Okay," admitted Andrew, "that's not my speciality. But what I mean is, we're all specialists."

"So what?" said John. It was hardly a question, but it got Andrew started—or something did.

"Well, let me tell you," said Andrew. "We all specialize, all of us fellows, don't we? We have to or we'd never get anywhere. We'd be second- or third-rate in our job if we didn't keep at it. How are you going to know more than the next guy if you spend your time reading poetry?

"Well," he spoke seriously, though I was uncertain how to take him, "this specialization is bound to go on more and more. Professor Cowley says so, too. It's the modern trend. All of us will have to work hard to keep up on our own specialities as they keep growing. Pretty soon Thomas's Fermi levels will be taught to freshmen. But look at the women."

"Ah," said John.

"Look at the women. They go to college and major in English or history or something, and after they graduate they get married and raise a family, and that's fine. Of course, some of them get jobs and work, but more likely they marry *us* and help us along.

"Well, that makes a good partnership. The women have the general education. We men have the specialized education. We need it for our jobs. They need their general education for their families, including us, so they can make us be civilized. There's just one more thing needed."

"And what's that?" Peter played up.

"That's to let the women run the country. Talk about votes for women; what you ought to do is to let the women do all the voting and take votes away from the men. The women are educated for voting. They've taken the general studies and the history and the philosophy, and they've got time to study up on elections so they can vote right, and there you are. Then the men can tend to their business and specialize, and the women can read about national affairs and go to political meetings and vote. It will give the men more time and give the women an important job to do, and everything will be done better. Division of labor, that's what it is. Adam Smith." I had not expected Andrew to hark back to Professor Cowley's talk at this particular moment.

"Do you mean the president and the senators will all be women?" objected Matthew.

"Oh, no. Same as now. Being a politician is a job, like being a lawyer or an auto mechanic. The women would do the voting, but they could vote for men to hold the political jobs. They do now," pointed out Andrew.

"Well, wouldn't everything be different?" asked Philip.

"Not very different," insisted Andrew. "Maybe better. There would probably be less graft and better schools and, since the ladies would have the benefit of a good general education, it would be harder for the politicians to put anything over on them."

"But . . . but . . . but. . . . " spluttered James.

"Sorry, I've got to go now. If you'll excuse me, sir." And Andrew actually got up and walked out.

He left the rest of us to talk about the percentage of time that ought to be devoted to general studies in the typical college curriculum and similar unexciting matters.

Should general studies occupy twenty percent, or twenty-five percent of the total time in four years? Professor Cowley had suggested some such division of time. Should general courses be elective and selected by the student or prescribed? Would a student in a particular subject—chemistry, for instance—take a democentric course in that same subject? Or, on the other hand, should a student from another department—say mathematics—be put into a chemistry course designed for a future chemist? Or should there be two separate courses, one for chemists and one for others; and, if so, who would teach the general democentric course, and how would the course be held up to some kind of standards? And how would the teacher of the democentric course gain recognition and promotion— this last was a subject of sharp interest to my seminar.

All these things we discussed in the remaining minutes, but we gave no serious consideration to Andrew's proposal. I wonder why.

17
A teacher's life

" ... a professor's life is quite a happy one," caroled Andrew as he pushed open the door, but he fell suddenly silent seeing that I had already started to introduce our speaker.

" ... and Professor Tuttle will talk to us today about 'A Teacher's Life'. Everyone knows, of course, that professors teach classes, and this is true as far as it goes, but it is only a part of the teacher's life. What else do you have in your future?

"I expect you already know Professor Tuttle as a scholar and a teacher. His classic book on *Network Synthesis* can be an example to both writers and teachers, as well as to mathematicians. Professor Tuttle likes to teach graduate and undergraduate classes in about equal parts, and he knows the facets of a teacher's life very well. Nevertheless he wants me to emphasize that his remarks today will be based only on his own experience."

Professor Tuttle started by drawing two axes on the blackboard. He marked them as shown.

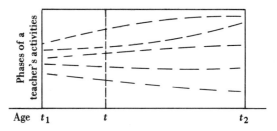

"Here, at t_1, you start teaching," and he marked a point at an early age. "Here, at t_2, you retire. At any point t in between," and he drew a vertical line, "your working time is divided among several jobs. How your time is divided depends partly on the school where you work, partly on your own interests, and partly on whether t is nearer t_1 or t_2.

"This vertical line indicates your various activities at age t. Let's draw a cross section of your activities like this," and he drew on the board another diagram with seven columns.

Teaching		Administration	Personal Education	Consulting	Advancement of Knowledge	
Class (group) teaching	Individual teaching		Special or general		Writing	Research
Subject matter	Seminars Research supervision Advising		Reading Talks Courses		Books Papers (less special)	Papers (special readers)
Absurd 12 / 0	0 / 0	0 / 0	0 / 0	0 / 0	0 / 0	0 / 12
Extreme 5 / 0	1 / 1	1 / 1	3 / 3	0 / 0	2 / 1	0 / 6

"Nearly everybody does some of most of these things. It would be absurd to say that anybody spent twelve hours a day teaching or twelve hours a day on research alone, and I have marked both of these rows of figures *absurd*.

"But someone might spend five hours a day on classroom teaching including preparation, plus a little time with individual students, plus some committee work or some other form of administration, together with a few hours on his own education by reading the literature or otherwise, and an hour or two on writing for publication. This might be an *extreme* amount of time to spend on classroom teaching, as I have indicated, but I expect it is not unheard of.

"On the other hand, another man in another school might spend most of his time—say six hours—on research and research writing and not do any classroom teaching at all. This is an extreme example, too, of another kind.

"It is important that there is feedback from each of these activities to every one of the others. That is why they all count as part of a teacher's work. The teacher might also, as a hobby, grow champion begonias, but I have not included this activity in the diagram because the feedback from begonias to teaching would be rather slight I imagine.

"Now each one of you must fill in your own numbers of hours in this tabulation. If you are young, and t is near t_1, the numbers under *Teaching* will no doubt be large. If t is nearer t_2, *Administration* will be greater, and possibly *Consulting* will be considerable, also.

Andrew sighed audibly. "Gosh, twelve hours a day. Is it for this that I gave up that eight-hour job at Edam Electronics?"

"Yes, the numbers in my diagram are on the basis of a twelve-hour day, but remember that this includes reading and studying and lectures that you attend and perhaps even concerts, too, under *Personal Education*. When these things are included in the twelve-hour day the estimate is probably not far wrong. In any case, it is up to you.

"I hope, however, that your columns for personal education will never be allowed to shrivel up. This is a danger that you will have to be careful to avoid, and it is up to you.

"Please notice that teaching, in these two columns over here," he pointed to the left-hand side of the diagram, "is a fairly complicated business. Of course you have to know what you are talking about, but you also have to be able to get it across. It has been said that 'Without good communication, scholarship is not enough.'

"However, any ordinarily good teacher will learn to communicate in his early years when t is not much greater than t_1. Communication is commonly done by lecture or by recitation or by tutorial meetings. The best ways to communicate naturally receive a large share of the attention of a young teacher.

"As the young teacher learns to communicate and so to impart factual information, he will also learn that two other important aspects of teaching are the encouragement of thinking and the encouragement of growth.

Information that the teacher gives to his students is of course limited. It is limited by time, it is limited by the maturity and ability of the students, and it is limited by the knowledge of the teacher. But the students must not remain permanently confined within these limits; they must learn to think for themselves. They must explore more deeply within the areas of their formal study, and they must also expand their understanding beyond the boundaries of their classroom learning.

"The life of the able teacher, then, includes not only *knowing* and *communicating* but also *encouraging*. Let me say that it is good, in ascending order of importance, when: *students learn, students enjoy learning, students seek to learn*.

"In our kind of work and perhaps in all kinds, the students must learn to solve problems, and if you can encourage them in problem-solving it will be most helpful. I have to ask myself, can problem-solving ability be taught? and I'm afraid I must answer no. But you can encourage it. All students, by solving problems, can improve their knowledge of the factual information you give them.

"In this connection may I speak of creative teaching. 'Creative' is a good word these days. I do not mean by creative teaching that the teacher is to be creative in new material and new courses, however desirable that may be. I mean that the student is to be creative, and here is no easy job for the teacher. You can only guide; you can watch for outstanding ability and give help and encouragement when possible.

"I like to think of three qualities for a good teacher as the three H's: *honesty, humility, humanity*. These are the qualities that will make it possible for you to be a truly effective teacher. These qualities must be developed through your lifetime. Perhaps humility is the most necessary of the three, and perhaps it is also the most rare.

"We are told that there are seven deadly sins. I forget what they are, but the two most deadly to teachers are *pride* and *anger*.

"A teacher is in danger of being proud of his great knowledge, but humility is more suitable than pride. Think of what you do *not* know. Moreover, even what you know today may not be true tomorrow.

"Remember that J. J. Thompson said, 'Any theory should be a *policy* and not a *creed*.' When Thompson discovered the electron and proposed that electricity was not merely a featureless fluid, there were a good many reputable scientists who disagreed with him. Perhaps they had allowed their theories to become their creeds. Throughout all science it is painfully easy to think of beliefs that have proved inadequate. As a recent example, everyone believed xenon to be an inert gas that formed no compounds until $XeFl_4$ appeared.

"The other sin that is deadly for teachers is anger. I do not necessarily mean the kind of anger that shouts and stamps; no teacher, I hope, would be so guilty. I mean even the smaller irritation that might be expressed in sarcasm or annoyance or querulousness. If a student comes to you for help don't brush him off: don't be rude. Don't say 'I have no time' because having time for students is the teacher's life. Don't say 'you are a dullard', for even if he is indeed thickheaded it does no good to say so. I suppose 'humanity' means treating a student as you would hope to be treated in his place.

"In any case in the part of your life that has to do with classroom teaching or individual teaching, anger—or even peevishness—is a sin.

"I am not saying that it isn't necessary sometimes to be firm. There are times to say no. There are times to call work inadequate. There are times to give a grade of D or even F. This is part of a teacher's life, too. A teacher is required to judge, and judging must sometimes be unpleasant.

"In order to judge as fairly as possible, we have to give examinations. Examinations and judgment are required, I suppose, by tradition, and our whole education system would be at a loss without grades. But there are two better reasons for examinations. For one thing, examinations are a stimulus for students. And for another, a good examination can be designed to teach."

A hand waved. "Sir," said Bartholomew, who was always interested in examinations, "I've heard that you sometimes give oral exams instead of written exams in courses. Could you tell us something about them?"

"Yes. I like to give oral examinations if I can. Any written examination is rigid. Whether it is a problem type of examination or multiple choice or essay, it is a fixed and passive sort of thing. An oral examination, on the other hand, can be flexible and adaptive and active. Giving an oral examination puts more requirements on the professor, for he must be flexible and adaptive, too. It takes experience."

"Oral exams take a lot more time, don't they?" asked Bartholomew.

"That depends. I think the best thing I can do is to quote Rudolf Panholzer, a professor who was here a few years ago. Dr. Panholzer tried both written and oral examinations, and he published a graph something like this." Professor Tuttle drew on the board.

"You see, if the number of students in a class is twenty or less, an oral examination is quicker for the teacher. This counts the time of making up

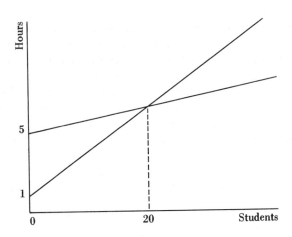

the questions and reading and marking the papers. If you have more than about twenty students in your class the written examination might be quicker."

"Isn't it hard to grade an oral exam?" Bartholomew inquired.

"Yes, I suppose it is harder to compare one student with another, but an oral examination should not consist of random questions without organization. Perhaps you can start by asking the same easy question of everyone, and if it is clear that a man can answer it, stop him. Go on to the next question, one notch harder, and keep on asking harder and harder questions until the man can't answer. Then you grade him according to the *difficulty* of the questions he can answer. This is different from the grade on a written examination, which depends on *how many* questions are answered.

"But here I am talking about examinations, which are always headaches, instead of the more pleasant parts of a teacher's life. One of the nicest parts of teaching is keeping up with new ideas. There are always new ideas in the subjects that we teach, and these keep the subjects from becoming stale to us. There are also new ideas of how to teach them. There are new possibilities for equipment and apparatus to use in demonstrations.

"Just this past year, for instance, in an undergraduate circuits course, the students and I have enjoyed demonstrations in which we could see electric waves on an oscilloscope, show their components on a panoramic frequency analyzer, and reproduce the waves from their components with a harmonic synthesizer. With these devices we can actually see the time domain and the frequency domain interchangeably.

"A new development that affects every teacher's life is the computer. Now that electronic digital computers are available to students and teachers we are no longer limited by the horse-work of calculation. Anything is now possible. We simply have a whole new world at our command. Linear or nonlinear, numerical or graphical, of any order or degree, we can do it now. If your classes don't know about this, they are missing something. It is up to you."

18

Publish

" 'Publish or perish'," said Dean J. M. Pettit, "is an unpleasant slogan that has caught on because there is a certain truth behind it. Taken literally or taken figuratively it is nonsense, but the truth is this: publication is the way to show your wares.

"Let's look at your own appointment to a faculty and your advancement in course of time to higher professorial ranks as these will be seen by the administrative people of your university. The dean, the provost or president, and the trustees or regents will have to decide whether you are the man they want, basing their decision largely on a written record of what you have done.

"What these administrative people know is that they want the men of their faculties to be outstanding. To be an outstanding professor means, among other things, that you must be expert, or at least becoming expert, in your subject. Your standing in your subject is best judged by other men who are themselves recognized experts in that subject, so their opinions will be sought. It is up to you to make their judgment favorable. The best way for you to be known is by publication of your work, so it is to your advantage to publish. It will improve your personal reputation.

"But there is another reason for publication, too, that will surely carry weight with your university administration. The welfare of the university itself depends on being known, and they hope for national visibility just as much as you want a good personal reputation. If there is good work going on in your university—good teaching, research at the cutting edge, up-to-date thinking and investigation—this can best be made known by the publications of the faculty. So here is another reason for you to publish: your administration will be pleased."

Dean Pettit paused for discussion, and Matthew grumbled, "It sounds to me as if the officials are awfully interested in reputation and visibility."

"Oh, no, not really," Dean Pettit explained. "The situation is that a judgment must be made. Is a certain man to be appointed to a faculty position or would someone else be better? Or perhaps a budget permits only one promotion, so will the promotion be yours or another's? How is a decision to be made? What can a fair-minded administrator best do?

"I suggest that the fairest means of weighing a man's technical competence is to ask for a judgment by his peers. If this man is publishing in science or in philosophy or in poetry, there will be plenty of other men in his field who can say that his work is good or bad.

"Of course, there are several kinds of publications, and while they are all good they are not all equally good. A research paper is one of the best, with several obviously good features. It shows that you are doing research with results worth publishing, that you are capable and informed; and from the point of view of the university, it shows that the atmosphere at your school is favorable to original work. A research paper is read by professors and others who are also doing research work in your field, and it helps build up your reputation—and that of your university—among the people who count most. A research paper is usually published in a refereed journal, and the mere acceptance of the paper shows that it has been judged by experts and found profitable.

"Publication of a book is good, too. Let us suppose that you have written a book that presents your subject in a new light, gives some new approach, or contains new material not previously published in a book. Let us suppose that it will be used in college classes as a text or reference book. Then its appearance shows that you are exceptionally well informed in your subject, that valuable work is being done at your school, and that your classes have the benefit of the latest thought. A book spreads your reputation and that of your university among professors and students everywhere. The publishing company sees to that, and while I certainly do not mean to say that a poor book never gets into print, I can assure you that a publishing company is not about to put a good many thousand dollars into a book until they are pretty sure that people will want to buy that book. It follows that manuscripts for books are reviewed with critical care.

"So the administrative officers of your university will be pleased and interested when you publish. They will note your publications and will consider the type of publication. . . . "

* * *

"There are *archival* journals," said Professor A. E. Siegman, "and *letters* journals and *news* journals, and there are *trade* journals, and *throwaways*, and journals that are various combinations of all these.

"The archival journals are kept in university libraries and private collections for permanent record; they include such periodicals as *Physical Review, Journal of Applied Physics, Journal of the Optical Society of America,* or *Proceedings of the Institute of Electrical and Electronics Engineers.* These are issued by the so-called learned societies. Sometimes the same societies issue other archival periodicals of more limited interest, too; each of the several professional or technical 'Groups' of the Institute of Electrical and Electronics Engineers publishes its own rather specialized *Transactions.*

"An archival journal is the right place for an important contribution to be published. However, papers are reviewed or *refereed* to determine suitability before they are accepted for publication, and the refereeing process is certain to take a long time; as much as six to nine months may elapse before a paper is printed. When someone has made a discovery that looks awfully important to him, he doesn't want to wait that long to tell everybody about it, so he writes a letter.

"For this purpose there are *Physical Review Letters, Applied Physics Letters,* and others; and journals publish these short, relatively informal letters very much more quickly. A letter may be refereed by only one man, and the delay is typically only about two weeks. It is expected, or at least hoped, that a letter will be followed up by an archival publication in course of time. The archival journals publish an occasional tutorial paper, too. This is a summary for the purpose of bringing the reader up to date in a particular subject.

"*The American Scientist* is put out by the research Society of the Sigma Xi and it rather specializes on tutorial papers. *Science* is issued by the American Association for the Advancement of Science and combines tutorials, archives, letters, and news.

"Publishing companies issue trade magazines such as *Electronics* or *Scientific American.* These have news and a sort of general interest type of tutorial article.

"I am best acquainted with the archival type of journal, for I am on the editorial board of the Proceedings of the IEEE. Let us suppose that you are writing a paper for some particular archival journal. It is assumed that you read that journal, too, and that you know that your paper is appropriate for their publication. Your typescript should be neat, of course, and in the style adopted by that journal. A booklet of instructions to authors is usually obtainable from the journal, giving suggestions about the number of copies, the form to be used, and such matters. They often print such instructions to authors in their January issues, too.

"How many of the papers submitted are printed? Well, a sample taken from one archival journal over a couple of years shows about half.

"Yes, papers should report original results only, except for tutorial articles that are frankly to review the work of a number of investigators. You must lean way over backwards to give credit for everybody else's work. Any suspicion that you are reporting what someone else has done is the surest way there is to be unpopular. There is a little verse that runs in my mind:

From Minsk to Pinsk my name is cursed;
They did the work, I published first.

* * *

"Books? Oh, yes," I said, and added with more enthusiasm than precision, "all teachers write books. So will you, no doubt."

"But sir," asked Philip, "why?"

"Is there much profit in writing a book?" asked Matthew. "I've heard it doesn't pay."

"Sour grapes," said John.

"Tell us, sir, how is it really?" urged Peter. "Why *do* teachers write books?"

"Well, Peter, there are a lot of reasons, really. Some teachers certainly write books for the money, and it is a fact that the royalty for a widely adopted textbook can be very substantial. In actual fact, books that sell do pay.

"But even a book that does not bring in much ready cash in royalties can still be counted on to have a most heartening effect on your dean. You will take the first two author's copies of your book to the head of your department and your dean, of course, and these will not be forgotten when the month of budgets and promotions rolls around.

"Another reason that was suggested the other day is that one way to have just the book you want for a class is to write it yourself. This is surely a reason for writing a book, although I'm afraid that this practice could result in a terribly large number of books with a pretty narrow market for each, and a lot of work with a minimum of profit. Perhaps this is what the Preacher in Ecclesiastes had in mind when he said: 'Of making many books there is no end; and much study is a weariness of the flesh.'

"Other authors write books to gain a scholarly reputation. Their books are likely to be very learned. Erasmus knew about these authors when he made Folly say (four and a half centuries ago), 'The Ones who write learnedly, for the verdict of a few scholars, seem to me more pitiable than happy, since they continually torture themselves: they add, they alter, they blot something out, they put it back in, they do their work over, recast it, they show it to their friends, they keep it for nine years; yet they never satisfy themselves. At such a price they buy praise—and that the praise of a handful. They buy it with so much loss of that sweetest of all things, sleep, so much sweat, so many vexations. Add also the loss of health, the wreck of their good looks, weakness of eyes or even blindness, poverty, malice, denial of pleasures, premature old age, and early death. The scholar considers himself compensated for such ills when he wins the approbation of one or two other weak-eyed scholars.'

"This was said, you understand, by Folly. Erasmus called his book *The Praise of Folly*. Folly thought more highly, she said, of ' . . . those who blacken paper with sheer triviality . . . For these are crazy in a far happier way. It is worth one's while to see how pleased they are with themselves when they are popular, and pointed out in a crowd.' Folly or no, this is a motive that counts, and Lord Byron added (some three centuries later), ' 'Tis pleasant, sure, to see one's name in print; a book's a book, although there's nothing in't.'

"An author hopes, too, that his work may go far beyond his personal sphere. Did you ever think that an author's book may be read by a hundred thousand pairs of eyes, whereas his lectures would not reach so many pairs of ears (even if he talked to a hundred students a year) for ten centuries—a whole millenium of lectures?

"Some authors, too, enjoy the additional glory of seeing their words, in print they cannot themselves read, going to students in far-off lands that they will never visit.

"An author, too, may hope for immortality. Edward Gibbon wrote his *Decline and Fall of the Roman Empire* with the hope, he says, that it might 'perhaps, a hundred years hence, still continue to be abused', and I am sure he would be gratified to know that now, after nearly two hundred years, it is indeed still read and doubtless still abused. 'In old age,' Gibbon wrote, 'the consolation of hope is reserved for . . . the vanity of authors who presume the immortality of their name and writings.' To this we can add the hope of Henry Fielding 'to be read with honor by those who never knew nor saw me, and whom I shall neither know nor see.'

"Then there are authors who write to promote a cause and to convert readers to their own beliefs. Here we may like to think of writers of history or politics, but let us not call the kettle too black, for I fancy that half the books on science and engineering (and I should not even dare to exclude my own) have bits of propaganda peering out between the lines. We may hope that the cause is good, as indeed it often is, and that the propaganda can therefore be called information.

"But of all authors, the happiest, I'm sure, are those who write for the fun of writing. It is better than chess or crossword puzzles. Do you know that Irish verse of a thousand years ago that says:

I and Pangar Ban my cat,
'Tis a like task we are at:
Hunting mice is his delight;
Hunting words I sit all night.

'Gainst the wall he turns his eye,
Full and fierce and dark and sly;
'Gainst the wall of knowledge I
*All my little wisdom try . . . ***

"So here are eight reasons for writing books:

1. To have a book for your own class
2. To get a bit of money
3. For academic advancement
4. To gain a scholarly reputation
5. For general recognition and acclaim
6. To extend your influence over the world and down the years

*This is a translation by Dr. Robin Flower from a commonplace book found in a Carinthian monastery. Reprinted by permission of the Estate of Dr. Robin Flower. (See *The Wandering Scholars* by Helen Waddell, Constable & Co. Limited, London, 1927.)

7. To support a cause or promote a hobby
8. Or just for the joy of writing.

Everyone who writes a book, of course, is urged on by several of these eight motives, and this is good. The public and the publishers might not be sorry to lose an author who wrote for only one of these reasons, but if you were to discourage all authors who like to see their names in print or like money or have a hobby, there would be a dearth of books.

"There," I concluded, "does that answer your question, Peter?"

"Yes, thank you," replied Peter, and he looked as if he could have done with less.

"It sounds to me like a speech," said Matthew fretfully.

"It was," I confessed.

19

Book

"I really would like to write a book some time," said Philip wistfully.

"Oh, I'm sure you will. Why," I said, "out of this many teachers... I wouldn't be surprised if several of you have ideas already. Would you like to talk about books? All right. Let's look at a book," and I picked up one that happened to be lying on the table, "let's look at it from title to index.

"I don't suppose you will ever really start a book by inventing a title. You really begin by knowing what kind of a book you want to write. Let's suppose it is going to be a textbook for class use. Alternatively, it might be a reference book or a research monograph for experts; and if it is either of these, the author has to worry most particularly about who, if anyone, is going to read it.

"But you pretty well know who is going to read a textbook. It is going to be used by students at a certain level in a certain department. Andrew here, for instance, might write a book for third-year mechanics students, or Thomas a graduate semiconductor book."

"Wow!" said Andrew.

"I'm afraid it isn't very likely," grieved Thomas.

"Well, it's up to you. Just remember that the way to write is to write. It has inelegantly been said that what you must do is to keep the seat of your pants on the seat of a chair. Don't let other things interrupt. When the time comes to write, write. Specifically, don't read. There comes a time when further reading is a hazard, not a help, and this is a subtle danger but deadly.

"You will know the general subject of the book before you begin writing. Will it be colloidal chemistry or general pyschology or photoelasticity? It must, of course, be a subject you know, and it had certainly better be a subject you teach. Above all, there must be a need for your book. You must feel the need, of course, and other teachers must feel the need, too, or you will be wasting your time on a book to blush unseen.

"Also—and this is more troublesome—you must not write what *was* needed or even what *is* needed, but write what *will be* needed soon. Then your work will be fresh and original, and by being a little ahead of the market, your book will be ahead of competition, too. Keep a little ahead—but not too much ahead or you will get credit rather than customers.

"After you know the subject of your book, it may be a long time before you select the actual *title*. But a title has to be chosen sooner or later, and the words of the title are perhaps the most important three words in the book. Three words? Well, if one or two words will say what must be said, so much the better: keep it short. Usually the general subject takes one word; for instance, most of my books have electric or electrical or electro-something in the title. Then in one or two words you can be specific: is it about circuits or lines or waves? And keep the title of your book a little different, if you can, from the titles of all other books.

"Think what people are going to call your book, for they won't often use the full title if it has more than one or two words. They will say *Tuttle's Synthesis*, or *Linvill's Models*, or *Skilling's Circuits*. And remember that libraries will catalog your book according to the words in the title. I once wrote a book that I wanted to call *Electricity Is a Long Dog*, which would really have been quite appropriate, but I suspect the publishers were afraid it would be catalogued among the dog stories, and these rather nice tales finally came out under the unexciting name of *Exploring Electricity*.

"After the title comes the *preface* and this is your chance to talk informally to the prospective user. Lots of people look at the preface first when they open a new book. I often do—don't you? Why was the book written, and what is new, and for whom is it intended? Here is the author's chance to encourage a possible customer to look further into the book and not just push it aside with a sigh. This is his chance and he had better not lose it; he has lost it indeed if he quenches some hopeful spark of interest with a tiresome preface. Perhaps the most common failing is to tell in a preface all that the book is not, instead of what it is. How could you better discourage a reader? On the other hand, lots of prefaces seem to me to promise so much that when you look into the book you wonder where it all is, and the book rather lets you down after that wonderful preface.

"At the *table of contents* you meet the prospective customer again. What you say here is limited to simple fact; you must say *what* but you can't say *why*. The question for the author is how much to put into his table of contents. Perhaps it gives a quick picture of the book, so that the possible customer can tell what is offered or the new owner can see the book's organization. How can you best give the picture that you want to show? It seems that you will surely need to list more than just the chapter headings, but you will hardly want a line in the table for every paragraph in the book.

"Next comes Chapter 1 of the *text*. The first thing your book must do is to gain the attention of your audience. This is a bit of a challenge to an author. I am supposing that you want the reader to be glad to read your book and not just look on it as an unpleasant necessity. I could talk at some length about the psychological advantage of making a book agreeable—but I won't. But do make the first paragraph attractive, and hold out a promise in the early pages of value to come.

"It seems to me that all those books that begin with a dull first chapter on definitions or something of the kind are throwing away an opportunity. Perhaps some well-disciplined students will grasp the nettle and slog on through such a swampy chapter, but don't you really find it easier to read a book that leads you beside the green pastures from the very beginning?"

" 'Beside the still waters', I think," corrected Matthew.

"Ah. Oh, yes, no doubt. Well, anyway, what I mean to say is that a time will come when the need for precise definitions will be seen, and then is the time for definitions to be given. When that time comes your careful definitions will be not only painless but genuinely interesting.

"The same thing is true of mathematics. It is possible, of course, to give vector algebra (for example) in the first chapter in a sort of vacuum, and just tell the students that they have to learn it because you say so; this can be done. But consider how much more pleasant it is, and how much better teaching, too, if you first show the awkwardness of the old mathematics in the development of your subject, then explain that here is an easier way, and only then present the helpful new mathematics.

"As you develop your subject through chapter after chapter of the *text*, see if you can prepare the way for each important new idea. Don't be obvious about it, but say just a word or two in advance—suggesting, fore-shadowing. Plan the notation and nomenclature that you are going to need, and see if you can make them familiar in earlier chapters. Especially, lead gradually to each new point of view, to each new concept. Then when the new concept comes, it won't seem hard at all but just a logical continuation of what the student has already been doing—which, indeed, we hope it is.

"Then after an idea has been introduced and illustrated and discussed, do not let it die. Find reasons in later pages to use it again. Work it into later chapters and keep the thought alive as long as possible. Here again do not be obvious, but let it seem to appear in the natural course of development.

"This is not logical, you say, and you are absolutely right. A good textbook is not just a logical ladder to be climbed, one dull step after another. After all, a book is written to help the reader. A terse and strictly logical book may be pleasing to the author and to others who already know the subject, but for a student it is likely to be fairly adamant."

"Fairly what?" asked John.

"Fairly hard to get into. It is said that Newton climbed to new heights and then, in writing his *Principia*, he knocked three-fourths of the rungs from his ladder so that anyone coming after him had to take giant steps. Well, perhaps Newton grew tired writing Latin with a quill, but you and I will do better to think of how to make the way interesting and perhaps challenging, but not discouraging.

"Young teachers sometimes like to be impressive by being obscure, or to cover their uncertainty as teachers by displaying their advanced knowledge of the subject. This is bad teaching, and it would be even worse writing.

"Always keep certain specific readers in mind as you write or you will wander. This is easy if you are writing a text for you can just keep thinking of your class of students.

"It is vastly better to teach the course while you are writing the book. For one thing, you can try the material on the students as you write, and every student will help you find any lack of clarity or ambiguity or possible mistakes. If it takes several years to write the book there will be several chances for the students to improve your work. Perhaps the students will help you see that the material is too repetitious or too much is left out or things are in the wrong order. If you ever find that you are not really telling your ideas to the class in the way you have written them, it is time to write the material over again. Don't be in *too* much of a hurry to finish."

BOOK 121

"How long does it take to write a book?" Andrew inquired.

"Well, it seems to take me about five years. But some authors turn them out more quickly, I believe."

"Some of the texts that we used to use at Camembert College looked like lectures notes just stuck end to end," remarked Matthew.

"I am afraid that is not impossible."

"It's quick, doing them that way," Matthew added.

"Someone has said (and I must apologize for his shocking language) that 'easy writing is damned hard reading.' "

"Yes," said Matthew.

"Finally, I hope you will finish your book in some proper way. A lot of books just seem to die of old age in the last chapter, and you only wish that it had happened sooner. Please remember that there is such a thing as structure. Here again, writing a textbook may be something like composing music. Perhaps that is why it is a pleasant thing to do.

"Now for practical questions. *How long* should the book be? A textbook should be written for either one or two semesters, having in mind the custom of the schools that will perhaps be using it.

"Should there be *summaries* at the ends of chapters? Yes, I think so. I have done books with and without, and I recommend summaries. Students can quickly review a summary to see if they are familiar with the important points of a chapter, and this is especially appreciated when an examination is looming.

"Should there be *examples* in the text? Of course, if the book has anything to do with solving problems. And *problems* for the students to work? If possible, yes; preparing problems for student homework is a pain to authors, but if your competition has problems and you have not, he sells and you don't.

"Should *answers* to problems be printed in the book? Well, some teachers like them and some don't. If you give answers to half or a fourth of your problems you keep everybody happy. But be exceedingly sure that your published answers are right. It is best to try problems on a class before printing the problems, and certainly before printing the answers. You'd be surprised until you have tried it how many misinterpretations a class can find for a problem that seems perfectly plain to you, and how many answers they can produce that are different from yours but not wrong.

"Do you want *appendices* at the back of your book? Reference material that is often needed can be convenient in an appendix. Don't forget that the end papers of the book, front and back, give the quickest possible reference.

"And at last we come to the *index*. When you are considering an entry for your index just try to think where some not very bright reader might look. Perhaps you will think of two or three possible entries; use them all. I have seen lots of books with too little index, and never a single book with too much. Have you?

"*Answer books* for teachers? *Teachers' manuals*? These items, published separately and not for students, have been growing more common in recent years and are often expected by customers. Publishers like to provide them to clinch an adoption. Nevertheless, I am dubious. If they get into the hands of the students at a college, the usefulness of your book at that college is finished. I wish it were not so; I don't quite know what to say.

"Should you enlist a *coauthor*? This depends on you; lots of writers do, but others prefer the freedom of working alone. I know a man who told a friend that he would rather have him as a friend than as a coauthor. I sympathize, for I can hardly conceive of myself writing in partnership with somebody else. Yet, for one reason or another, and some of them good, books are often done jointly.

"Now what about a *publisher*? Naturally you want a publisher with representatives covering all the domestic markets and as many foreign ones as possible, a publisher active in your own subject. Even more, you want a publisher who does good work, a publishing house with fidelity, and a publishing company of people whom you like and respect. The character and personality of the people are much more important than the written contract you sign. You will trust the publisher a great deal; indeed, you will have to, and this is all right; in my experience all honorable publishers do far more for the author than is guaranteed in the contract.

"The rate of *royalty*? Well, that will certainly follow the terms of the contract. How much you get is fairly standard under a given set of circumstances, depending on the nature of the book and whether it is likely to be profitable; but check around if you are doubtful. Remember when you check that list or retail price is higher than the publisher's price to a bookstore by about twenty percent on a textbook. Remember also that 'advances' to an author have to be repaid from royalty. The form in which a publisher will accept a manuscript is often important to an author, too. Will the publisher accept a manuscript in some good duplicated form rather than in original typewriting? Most publishers prefer to have the necessary drawings for cuts made at their own expense—but ask. Foreign sales are pleasant for an author but not very profitable. When everything is taken into account it is possible that one publisher will offer substantially more than another, but it is not likely. If it looks as if there is a great difference, ask yourself why.

"The *price* at which your book will be sold is set by the publisher. Is it a textbook for undergraduate students, with each adoption calling for hundreds of copies? Then the price will be a cent or two a page, depending somewhat on the amount of artwork and the number of equations, and perhaps you will sell ten thousand copies in the life of the book—or perhaps a hundred thousand.

"Is the book for small graduate classes or a reference book for a few engineers, mathematicians, chemists, or others working at jobs? Then the sale will be smaller and the price higher. Perhaps one or two thousand copies will be sold altogether, and the price will have to be three or four or five cents a page.

"Paper covers? Well, a paperback book can be sold about two dollars cheaper than a hardback, but paper covers get dog-eared pretty quickly.

"When I was first writing a book," I remarked, "Dr. Terman (who spoke to us the other day) gave me some good suggestions, which I shall now pass on to you. His *Radio Engineering* was a new book then, and I expect you know it now, for not many technical books have been so successful. He said:

> *Don't* waste time with a "scissors and paste" book, using second-hand material that you just rearrange.
>
> *Don't* be thinking of what your highbrow friends will say about your book; think of the great numbers of students and teachers in all the colleges around the country.
>
> *Don't* try for perfection. If you don't let go of your manuscript because you feel it isn't quite perfect yet, you'll never publish it.

"We looked at my manuscript, too, and he urged:

> *Don't* fill the pages with equations. Too many equations and too little writing make it hard to read.
>
> *Have enough drawings* and diagrams so that a person opening the book at random will probably see one.

"I have tried to follow Dr. Terman's suggestions, and I recommend them to you."

"Should every course have a textbook?" Philip asked. "I know Professor Vennard said so; do you agree?"

"Why, yes," I replied. "Books are a great help to both students and teachers. A student who has a subject all carefully presented to him in a book is clearly better off than a student who doesn't, other things being equal. And then in later years that student will naturally turn to his old familiar textbook when he is faced with a problem, knowing that he will understand the words and symbols and perhaps even find his own notes scribbled in the margins.

"A teacher is better off with a book, too, for he has ever so much more freedom. He can use his class meetings for supplementing, emphasizing, showing examples, recitations, or for whatever purpose he wishes, knowing that his students can read the book for themselves.

"Some teachers complain that no book yet written contains all the recent developments they want for their advanced classes. These unfortunate teachers must of necessity get along with duplicated notes, I suppose, or even with student transcription of lectures, unless the teacher himself can write the book he needs.

"In general a teacher can plan a course in either of two ways. Sometimes a teacher feels that the right way is to decide what ought to go into a course and write an outline or something. Then he searches for a book that comes reasonably close to fitting his outline, and he tries to make the best of what is available.

"Other teachers, and I include myself, prefer to select a really good book on the desired subject and follow the presentation of the book. I believe that the advantage of using the best book far outweighs the disadvantage—if it is a disadvantage—of accepting the author's organization. Indeed, I am only too glad to have the author organize the subject for me."

"Sir," asked Bartholomew, "are ordinary books about to be replaced by programmed books?"

"This is a question that I have followed pretty carefully in the last few years, and I have come more and more to question whether there is any great difference between a careful textbook that can be read without requiring a teacher to explain what it means, and an efficient programmed book that takes into due account the maturity and quick intellect of a college student. It seems to me that the two forms could not be very different."

"What about a teaching machine?"

BOOK 125

"Ah, yes; a teaching machine. Did I ever show you Dr. Tuttle's clipping about *The Ultimate Teaching Machine*? No? Well, . . . " and I riffled through the papers in my notebook. "Here it is—*Learn with BOOK*, by R. J. Heathorn.*

A new aid to rapid—almost magical—learning has made its appearance. Indications are that if it catches on, all the electronic gadgets will be so much junk. The new device is known as Built-in Orderly Organized Knowledge. The makers generally call it by its initials, BOOK.

Many advantages are claimed over the old-style learning and teaching aids on which most people are brought up nowadays. It has no wires, no electric circuits to break down. No connection is needed to an electricity power point. It is made entirely without mechanical parts to go wrong or need replacement.

Anyone can use BOOK, even children, and it fits comfortably into the hands. It can be conveniently used sitting in an armchair by the fire.

How does this revolutionary, unbelievably easy invention work? Basically BOOK consists only of a large number of paper sheets. These may run to hundreds where BOOK covers a lengthy program of information. Each sheet bears a number in sequence, so that the sheets cannot be used in the wrong order. To make it even easier for the user to keep the sheets in the proper order they are held firmly in place by a special locking device called a "binding."

Each sheet of paper presents the user with an information sequence in the form of symbols, which he absorbs optically for automatic registration on the brain. When one sheet has been assimilated a flick of the finger turns it over and further information is found on the other side. By using both sides of each sheet in this way a great economy is effected, thus reducing both the size and cost of BOOK. No buttons need to be pressed to move from one sheet to another, to open or close BOOK, or to start it working.

BOOK may be taken up at any time and used by merely opening it. Instantly it is ready for use. Nothing has to be connected up or switched on. The user may turn at will to any sheet, going backwards or forwards as he pleases. A sheet is provided near the beginning as a location finder for any required information sequence.

*Reprinted by permission of PUNCH, London.

A small accessory, available at trifling extra cost, is the BOOKmark. This enables the user to pick up his program where he left off on the previous learning session. BOOKmark is versatile and may be used in any BOOK.

The initial cost varies with the size and subject matter. Already a vast range of BOOKs is available, covering every conceivable subject and adjusted to different levels of aptitude. One BOOK, small enough to be held in the hands, may contain an entire learning schedule. Once purchased, BOOK requires no further cost; no batteries or wires are needed, since the motive power, thanks to the ingenious device patented by the makers, is supplied by the brain of the user.

BOOKs may be stored on handy shelves and for ease of reference the program schedule is normally indicated on the back of the binding.

Altogether the Built-in Orderly Organized Knowledge seems to have great advantages with no drawbacks. We predict a big future for it.

20
Research

"I can tell you," I said in introduction, "that Professor Paul Kirkpatrick is a certified good teacher, for in addition to my own opinion we have the judgment of the American Association of Physics Teachers. He was awarded the Oersted medal for excellence in teaching at a joint meeting of the American Physical Society and the American Association of Physics Teachers.

"Professor Kirkpatrick made some good remarks to the two societies assembled in New York on that occasion, and I am hoping that he will give us some of the same comments this afternoon. He may have other things to say to us, too, but he could hardly talk about anything of greater moment in academic life than the relationship of teaching and research.

"Of course you will recognize that Professor Kirkpatrick is himself a research man as well as a teacher. A good deal of his work has been done on x-rays, and I think he is now interested in stellar x-rays. These are best observed above the earth's atmosphere, and nearly all that is known about such radiation has been learned from rocket observations. What I mean to say is that he speaks of research and teaching as an expert in both. Professor Kirkpatrick."

"First I should like to say a word about our professional neighbors, the research people." Professor Kirkpatrick spoke quickly and firmly, with a light touch. "Of course a researcher is often a teacher with his research hat on, but there are many teachers who do not possess such a hat. And there are some research men who do no teaching.

"This is a fairly modern problem. Today research is so generally accepted as one of the functions of an institution, if not the main function, that you may find it hard to realize that even in the later nineteenth century the eminent presidents, Eliot of Harvard, White of Cornell, and Gilman of Johns Hopkins, declared that teaching was much more important than investigation. At the beginning of the present century the leading enthusiasts for research were the young physicists home from Europe with their dazzling German PhD degrees, but they were few in number for a big country.

"Here and there a little research came into the universities. It would be ridiculous to claim that it did not compete with the teaching function. It is told that when Michelson was asked how he managed to get so much good research done he replied, 'By neglecting my students.' (That's a practice that did not die with Michelson.)

"When teaching moved over to make room for research—around 1900 and thereafter—some educators and scientists who believed strongly in both activities tried to play down the mutual interference effects. These coexistentialists were heard advancing three propositions, and I repeat them.

First, every good research man is *ipso facto* a superior teacher.

Second, it is not possible for a nonresearch man to be a superior teacher.

Third, the partnership of research and instruction is always mutually beneficial.

"I don't think that these assertions were inductions from any real observations; they were, I believe, just articles of faith—adopted, not derived. I am afraid the weight of the observations is against them all, but they were attempts—wistful perhaps—to deal with a real problem that is still unsolved: the problem of promoting the mutually helpful coexistence of instruction and investigation in science.

"Since these three claims may still be heard occasionally, we will take a closer look at them. The first one was strongly worded by President David Starr Jordan, who said, 'I very much doubt if any really great investigator was ever a poor teacher.' Seemingly President Jordan had not heard of the case of Willard Gibbs, Yale's research giant, who has been called the most distinguished American mathematical physicist of his day, known for the phase rule and for vector analysis. He is said to have failed so completely as a teacher that there was a movement to replace him. We have all been graduate students, and most of us can remember sitting before at least one honored—and justly honored—research scientist who, for one reason or another, was unsuccessful in the classroom. Possibly he didn't care for people; perhaps he was just naturally inarticulate; it may be that he was bored with teaching and considered it an unimportant part of a job that he had accepted mainly to be able to do his research. Fortunately a scholar of this type no longer needs to suffer in the classroom. Not the physics classroom. He can now get a better job requiring the full-time use of his highest talents.

"I am not suggesting that there is any *negative* correlation between effectiveness in research and in teaching, but only that the positive correlation is a long way from unity. The brilliant critic José Ortega y Gasset wrote, 'I have lived close to a good number of the foremost scientists of our time, yet I have not found among them a single good teacher.' To me this is incredible testimony. I have also lived close to some top scientists and I am sure there were top teachers among them, judged according to any definition or test you might devise.

"I turn to the claim that a man not doing research or not eager to do research can never be a superior teacher. The affirmative argument holds that one never really understands the inwardness of physical phenomena, the treachery of glib but plausible explanations—never grasps the reasons behind the reasons until he digs clear to the bottom of extant knowledge and then a little deeper. This argument sometimes maintains that book learning is fine if you want verbal knowledge, but research people are doers of the word and not hearers only. The superior teacher should have buried himself in the physical mysteries and drawn out the truth with eyes, ears, tactual nerve endings, and the sense of smell.

"Now I do think that experience in research has improved many a teacher's comprehension of the nature of science and greatly deepened his understanding of specific problems. But science is long, life is short, and research is narrow. There is not time enough to master the whole of physics through direct research experience, and the detailed insight that a man has time to secure in this way will rarely be passed on to his students unless he is giving a seminar in his research specialty. Any teacher of a *general* physics course who devotes more than fifteen minutes of lecture time to his own research may be suspected of egotism.

"The method of the theorists—that is, mastering science by reading literature instead of meters—is open to every teacher who lives near a library to the degree permitted by his mentality, his temperament, and of course his time commitments. If his thinking leads him to formerly unrecognized truths, then he is a research man, but his teaching is benefited whether his study has this by-product or not. The teacher who chooses this method of learning has no reason to feel (I should say) that his colleague who reads meters has a superior pipeline to the sources of enlightenment.

"To point out that many research men are superb teachers and draw the conclusion that the doing of research *per se* made them that way is to commit a logical fallacy too elementary to dissect before this audience.

"Now a word about the third axiom that I quoted—the statement that the association of instruction and research necessarily benefits both. It is easy to point out that each depends upon the other, for it was research that gave the teacher something to teach; but without the teacher's support, research would die out tomorrow for a lack of trained workers. Yet beyond this broad interdependence some individual scientists have found the combination advantageous in their own lives. Hans Christian Oersted discovered electromagnetism while in the very act of demonstrating before an audience. Sir J. J. Thomson writes in his autobiography that the bright, inquiring minds of students kept him from settling into fixed mental postures, while their questions sometimes stirred him to think thoughts conducive to discovery.

"Well, everyone wishes it might always work this way, but does it? I think not. In the life of a university department the interests of research and of teaching are competitors. I don't mean to say that *people* within a department must necessarily engage in controversy with each other in the promotion of their rival activities, though this may happen. I just mean that the activities themselves are in necessary conflict in any department which thus seeks to serve two masters. These activities compete for room space, for the working time of staff members, including mechanicians and secretaries, for funds, and for the control of faculty appointments.

"If you will pardon my own unimportant case history, I got into research in the era of love and string and sealing wax. I outlived the string and the sealing wax but love lingers on. In my experience the demands of research and of teaching have been in continual conflict for nearly forty years, and I cannot remember that either function ever helped the other. Many a demonstration would have been better prepared and many a student better served if the urgency of some situation in the research laboratory (and the fascination of it) had not pulled in that direction. On the other hand, the continuous concentration that a research dilemma can demand was often broken up by the class bell. I suspect that there are hundreds of scientific men who could give the same testimony. This is not a situation that we can take any satisfaction in but is just one of the facts of academic life.

"Now another category of people with whom we deal is the students. These are our best customers, and I don't see how we could ask for better ones; they crowd in upon us with their immense demand for our product; they pay their money and accept what we give them—most uncritically; and they seem especially pleased when we give them short weight. I mean I know of no case in an American college where the students have protested the announcement of a holiday or where they have organized a demand for longer and harder problem sets.

"I believe that in many universities and institutes we have been taking advantage of the student's poor business sense and giving him less than his money's worth. I am thinking of the institutions of high repute where a part of the teaching—indeed, the most direct and personal part of it—is entrusted to amateur teachers and often to absolute beginners. This is the unmentioned skeleton in the closet of higher education. Uncritical as students are, some of them do think it strange—and they have told me so— that they have had only trained and experienced teachers in the free public schools but have had some teachers who were complete novices in prestigious high-tuition institutions.

"Many teachers are quite outside the system I am criticizing, for many liberal arts colleges do not have any graduate students around, and therefore the teachers have to do the teaching. I have long felt that this is a real point of superiority for the four-year colleges, and it may have had something to do with the demonstrated ability of some such institutions to surpass big universities in the preparation of students for graduate training in the sciences.

"Teaching assistantships in physics used to be justified as a means of subsidy for the graduate students. It is not certain that the tuition-paying undergraduate would go along with this defense, but it is certain that the graduate student of today does not need this assistance as greatly as did his predecessors. There has been a vast increase in the number of agencies competing for a chance to aid him. Is it too much to hope that the universities will some day relieve the graduate student of his teaching duties, put a better-qualified teacher in his place, and then—in case the graduate student really wants to learn about college-level teaching—do something serious about training him?

"I have called the student a customer, but I really think of him as a client. We offer counsel that the client may be persuaded to act upon. But getting the client to respond and comply requires a professional relationship that I shall call *rapport*. It is about as important to the teacher's success as is his knowledge or his apparatus. It becomes more difficult to achieve this rapport as enrollments go up. For the master with a few disciples, rapport is easy; for the radio or TV teacher, it is impossible. Most of us stand somewhere in between. Rapport means knowing the state of ignorance of the student and of the class, so that one does not explain the obvious nor yet the incomprehensible. A teacher must sense what goes on in the minds of his students or he will not know what to say to them. Rapport means knowing the student's question as soon as he opens his mouth to ask it. When we are greatly surprised by the results of an examination, finding that the class has done far better or worse than we expected, we stand convicted of faulty rapport. When we are astounded by a student's ignorance, we reveal that we have not been on the job; and the teacher who indulges in sarcasm about a student's stupidity is unnecessarily exposing his own.

"Once upon a time a university known to me invited a learned man to serve as visiting professor, and after a few weeks it became evident through student complaints that the visitor's lectures were not going over. The department head then discussed the situation with the visitor and suggested that he adjust his presentation to the immaturity of the class. The visiting professor took the suggestion as an affront to his honor, and with a show of dignity he said, 'What you ask is impossible! *I* have standards.'

"Ever since that experience the department in question has checked every candidate to make sure that they didn't invite another man who had standards.

"Finally, I ask your pardon for my many statements that should have been preceded by the words, 'It is my opinion that. . . . ' When exact scientists voice their views in the debatable areas of the arts or of human relations they need to be guided by the three classic rules for courting a woman, of which, as you may recall, the first is—be bold. The second rule is—be bold; and the third is—but be not *too* bold.''

The applause by my seminar was unusual. However, it seemed that Thomas had failed to understand. "Wouldn't it be better, then," he asked, "if universities quit doing research?"

"Not at all." Professor Kirkpatrick spoke even more crisply than usual. "The university is the natural home of research. But it takes money, or at least it does now. When my predecessor, D. L. Webster, first came to Stanford he would survey the university junk yard for raw material before planning his research equipment. But now we have contracts, and 'contract' is a new word in the last twenty-five years; it means 'a way to get money out of the government'.

"Research these days takes manpower, too, as well as equipment. Faculty men work in teams with research students, PhD candidates, and technicians; and all these take money. Also they take space. For these reasons it may be better for small colleges to leave research to the universities. In America, fifty universities give ninety percent of the PhD's in physics, but some small colleges give better MS degrees than these fifty big universities do. Maybe the preoccupation of university teachers with research has something to do with the reason."

"Do faculty men have time to do both research and teaching?" asked Philip.

"Some do. They can usually find time if they want to. Suppose a man teaches two or three classes; that would be six or nine hours a week in class. Office hours and so on might bring his total time with students up to eighteen hours a week. Then preparation takes time. But what else does he do in fifty hours or more a week?

"He can write books, which might make him rich. Or he can write journal articles, which might make him famous. Or he can do research, which might satisfy his curiosity and will surely help him get promotion.

"He'll have to spend some time with correspondence, and help entertain Visiting Firemen, and occasionally pay visits himself.

"He'll have to do something with university administration, though he probably won't want to. Most professors are ambivalent; they don't like bosses, but they don't want to do the boss's work themselves. Hence there are committees. Some faculty men love committees; these are public-spirited people, and they become deans. It just isn't possible to get along without department chairmen, deans, presidents or whatever you call them. But don't put the cart before the horse. The purpose of an administrator is to help the professor do his job."

"And the professor's job is teaching?" suggested Peter.

"Teaching *and* investigation. A man from Mars looking over our universities would no doubt say that these were the things that counted."

"Can you tell us," pursued Peter, "how anybody can tell if a teacher is doing his job well? How can he or anyone else know whether he is an effective teacher?"

"Yes, I can tell you," replied Professor Kirkpatrick, "but I don't know how you can apply this yardstick to any particular man. A good teacher is a teacher whom the A students will consider to have been a good teacher five years later."

"Er . . . ah . . . what did you say?" John gasped.

Professor Kirkpatrick repeated his formula and added, "But five years later the A students will have vanished, and the professor may have evaporated, too—and in any case the most you can find out by this test is how good a teacher he was five years ago."

"Yes, I see," said Peter. "But what can we do to try to make ourselves good teachers?"

"Well, there are some scientific facts that we ought to know. We who are in the exact sciences don't have as much respect as we should have for our colleagues across the Quad in psychology and education. They have some scientific knowledge, too. When we are stuck in a chemistry problem we go to the chemists. When we get beyond our depth in mathematics we know mathematicians who will throw us a rope. I think that sooner or later all teachers are going to have to agree that some kind of scientific basis is possible for what they are trying to do, and I wish we were getting ready for that time now."

21

From across the quad

"There are all kinds of ways of teaching a class," said Professor Hilgard. "Some like informality, but some get fussed by it. Some do best with regular lectures, and others prefer the give and take of small groups like this. It doesn't make much difference."

Professor E. R. Hilgard had come at my invitation to talk to the seminar on learning. His studies of psychology and his books were known throughout the world, and the psychology of learning was a major area of his work.

Professor Hilgard smiled broadly at the seminar as he sat on the edge of the table. "McKeachie at Michigan has studied all kinds of teaching methods, with big classes and small classes, lectures, recitations, seminars, and everything you can think of. He found that any small differences resulting from these obvious factors were overshadowed by a greater difference from some more subtle cause. At first there was no clear pattern, but as the work developed it appeared that the effectiveness of teaching depended on whether the teacher liked the students, which was reflected in whether the students liked the teacher. Compared to this, the more obvious factors didn't seem to correlate strongly."

"I suppose it is not surprising, in view of McKeachie's conclusions, that a graduate student of mathematics who got his doctorate here with us a while ago by making a comparison of teaching methods found a similar result. He taught one section of a math class himself, using the most approved methods, developing the students' insight and creativity, and

135

leading them to think for themselves in seeking solutions for mathematical problems; and he was a good teacher. At the same time another section of the class was taught by a retired army colonel who thought well of military methods. He was liked and respected by his class, but he saw to it that assignments were completed, homework was done, and lessons were learned. He and the younger man contrasted in just about every way. Yet at the end of the semester the two sections of the class were compared by taking identical examinations—and there was no measurable difference between them.

"Well, all this seems to show that the method of teaching doesn't really make so very much difference. You might think that this is my conclusion and that I have finished and will now go away. But I haven't really finished, and I am not going away just yet.

"Two kinds of learning that are often compared or contrasted are habit formation and insight. A great deal of work on habit formation has been done by B. F. Skinner at Harvard. He talks about *operant conditioning*. Learning results from reinforcement of correct decisions. The learner, whether he is a person or a pigeon or a monkey, is rewarded when he moves even a little in the wanted direction, and not rewarded when he doesn't.

"The learner, according to Skinner's theory, starts at what is called the operant level. How he gets to the operant level, by instinct or training or experience, is the source of a good deal of controversy, but this is really no part of Skinner's theory.

"I like to bring a pigeon to one of my psychology classes to show how well the theory works. The operant level in this case means that the pigeon can walk about and peck at things he sees. I want to teach him to peck at a black spot on a card.

"My pigeon is a naïve and unsophisticated pigeon; he has never been trained before. Also he is a hungry pigeon because he hasn't been fed much lately, so to begin I give him a few grains of wheat or something just to make him happy.

"Well, the pigeon is on a table, and the card with the black spot is on the table, too. The pigeon is rather restless because he's hungry, so he keeps walking around. When he walks toward the card with the spot I give him a little reward—this is called *reinforcement*. Pretty soon he walks right up with his breast against the card, and he finds that when he does that he gets fed, so he stays there. Pigeons just naturally peck, so pretty soon he pecks at something. If he pecks at the card I reinforce his behavior with a little food, so he tries it again and it works. But about that time I become more particular, and he doesn't get any reinforcement unless he pecks the black spot. This doesn't take long, and pretty soon he's pecking away like a woodpecker. It only takes about two minutes to train a pigeon to peck at a spot.

"Then the pigeon's behavior can be shaped. You can teach him to peck at a big spot and not a little one, or a little spot and not a big one. It is not generally known, but some early experimental models of missiles were guided by a pigeon who rode in the nose and pecked when the cross hairs were not on the right spot. This was horribly nonmechanized and was soon superseded, but it worked.

"There are two things to be noted about training the pigeon. First, you begin reinforcing his behavior when he first moves in the right direction even though he has never made a successful peck. This kind of thing is hard for teachers to do. A teacher with a class of children is likely to be impatient of any imperfection and will only reward the right answer to a problem. But operant conditioning would reward any move in the right direction, even if it were still a long way from the goal. At the beginning of the term a student might be rewarded with a good grade or a pat on the back for just setting up the problem right, but later in the term there would be no reward unless he carried on and got the right answer.

"The second point is that punishment is never used. A reward can be given or withheld but there is no punishment. This is not done out of kindness, but because reward is more effective than punishment. Perhaps the reason is that punishment often has unwanted by-products; one obvious result can be that punishment may not encourage a child to work for a right answer but merely to hide a wrong answer.

"A reward for getting the right answer doesn't have to be tangible such as food or money; it can be an encouraging word, or a good grade, or approval by the teacher, or social approval. In the end the reward gets to be approval by the learner himself; he rewards and reinforces himself by thinking well of his own effort and approving what he has done. This is sometimes called working toward a standard of excellence. Then the pats on the back and the better grades and the raises of salary are no longer needed. But maybe they still help.

"An important part of operant conditioning is what is called the schedule of reinforcement. Except at the very beginning you don't reinforce every correct move. When a mother is teaching her child to look both ways before crossing the street she gives him a good word and a pat on the back when he does—but not every time. In the first place, it isn't necessary to reinforce every time, and in the second, it is better not to. The child will begin to expect it and won't look both ways unless his mother is along to give him a reward. When reinforcement is given sometimes but not always, the child will begin to reward himself for good behavior when he does look both ways; and this is what you want because it keeps him looking both ways even when he's alone.

"Another important fact is that the most effective reward is the least that will maintain the desired result. You might think that a big reward would give a big reinforcement, but this isn't so. A small reward is better, provided it is enough to maintain the desired result. Then self-reward will the sooner replace reinforcement by a teacher.

"The moral of this is: in teaching don't use grades too much. Self regard will do better, and social approval is a very strong reward. Besides, low grades tend to be a form of punishment.

"Teaching machines work on the Skinner theory of learning." (I had forgotten to tell the seminar that Professor Hilgard was an authority on teaching machines and also on programmed books.) "Teaching machines have several good features.

"For one thing, a teaching machine rewards everyone. When the learner gives the right answer to a question there is an immediate reward. Perhaps a light turns on to indicate that the learner was successful and may now go to the next lesson; something like that is arranged to give reinforcement. Such rewards may not come as frequently to the poor student as to the brighter one, but at least they do come. In an ordinary class, words of encouragement or reinforcements for the less bright students are likely to be spread awfully thin.

"Notice that a teaching machine does not use punishments. It does not, for instance, flash a green light if you're right and a red light if you're wrong. It just flashes brightly when you're right.

"It is always distressing to a teacher to see how slowly a machine has to go. It takes amazingly short steps and proceeds at a snail's pace. But this is true of any kind of programmed learning, and as a matter of fact, any good teacher probably goes just as slowly. A teacher goes more slowly than he realizes probably, and he puts in a lot of repetition and a lot of redundancy. The retired colonel who teaches mathematics undoubtedly goes over and over his subject by means of examples and problems, and he gives quizzes and examinations on what he has taught. A lot of repetition is pretty standard in any way of teaching.

"Now," said Professor Hilgard, "I think this might be a good time to stop awhile for questions or comments."

"Sir," Andrew had been looking disturbed for the last few minutes. "Sir, don't you think that punishment is pretty effective sometimes? I remember times when I should have known something and didn't, and I just got it *burned* into me. Things like that I'll never forget."

"Well, maybe." Professor Hilgard might have been considering the question. "But it didn't make you like the subject or the teacher any better, did it? I suppose it really depends a good deal on the way the student reacts. Some people have a high degree of anxiety about failure, and in others the anxiety level is low. High-anxiety people do best if they are just left alone, but maybe it is good for low-anxiety people to be stirred up a bit now and then. Punishment can make some people afraid of the teacher and the subject and can even cause a neurotic dread. In any case it is an observed fact that training takes place faster if there are rewards but no punishments.

"It might seem that there was not much difference between hope of success and fear of failure, but actually these aren't the same at all. One of the tests that Atkinson has used at Michigan is interesting in this connection. It is a ring-toss game, in which you win by tossing a ring over a hook in the wall. Michigan students were asked to play this game, and they could choose how far they wanted to stand from the hook. Actually it was this distance from the hook that was interesting to the psychologist giving the test. Some wanted to stand quite close, some halfway back, and some all the way back where they missed nearly every time.

"The way it worked out was that those who were pretty good at ring tossing and had low anxiety about failure chose to stand about halfway back where success was difficult but quite possible. They didn't mind missing part of the time if they could win part of the time. Their hope of success was greater than their fear of failure, and the challenge attracted them.

"On the other hand, those who were just as good at ring tossing but had high anxiety about failure showed a tendency to stand close where they could win nearly every time, or else at so great a distance that they would probably miss. With these high-anxiety people, fear of failure was greater than hope of success; and they either ensured against failure by standing close, or they stood so far away that there was no stigma attached to missing. Missing from so far away wasn't really failure.

"This same tendency to avoid risk was found by Atkinson, too, in other decisions, such as the selection of courses by students in college. High-anxiety people are a little more inclined to take either courses that are easy or those that are known to be very hard, rather than to accept the challenge of a moderately hard course.

"On another level, a chimpanzee is an anxious kind of animal. Chimpanzees can be trained with great success to do remarkable things, but the training has to be done entirely by rewarding and reinforcing their successes. If you punish a chimpanzee he just freezes up and becomes neurotic and probably aggressive.

"On the other hand the current issue of *Science** has an article by Bertrand on 'Training Without Reward' that tells how macaque monkeys are taught to pick coconuts in southeast Asia. They are punished for failure but never rewarded for success, and their trainer doesn't even feed them. Bertrand tells about it, but then he concludes by saying that the training system works but might work better if rewards were used."

Professor Hilgard paused and looked around, inviting other questions.

"A while ago," James said, "you spoke of the kind of learning that requires insight. This must be a different kind of learning."

"Well, yes, to some extent," replied Professor Hilgard.

"Does this mean creativity? And can creativity be taught?"

"Can creativity be taught? Well, a good many people think so, but it's hard to be certain. Maybe all a teacher can do is to be careful not to damage or squelch a natural creative ability. 'Creativity' is a good word these days, and there have been a lot of studies of creativity and intelligence. Some of these are rather interesting."

"But sir," put in John, "what *is* creativity?"

"It is sometimes considered to be a *divergent* kind of thinking, an effort made outward in all directions to seek the solution of a problem. Intelligence is *convergent*, with all ability directed inward toward achieving the solution of some well-defined problem.

"Creativity is tested for in various ways. One simple test is to ask a man to list all possible uses for a brick. A brick can be used for a paperweight or the end of a bookcase, to warm a bed, and so on, but you don't count its ordinary uses for the construction of a wall or a path. As another test you can ask for uses for a newspaper: to light a fire or make a hat, and so on.

"Well, using this kind of test for creativity and an IQ test for intelligence, it is found that the correlation you get depends very greatly on the degree of intelligence. In the population who come in the lowest 25 percent of intelligence, there is close correlation between intelligence and creativity. In the middle half of the population there is less correlation, but there is some. In the top quarter, where the IQ is something like 125, there is no correlation at all between intelligence and creativity. This top quartile is the population group that might be able to graduate from a good university.

"It's hard to suggest how creativity can be taught, but there is a general feeling that it can at least be encouraged. I would suggest that when a student shows a little creativity he could be rewarded. His creative idea might be remarked and celebrated a little, even if it was really a pretty small achievement.

"Actually, teachers are not much inclined to reward creativity. In general they prefer high IQ to high creativity. The high IQ students do well in class work, and they tend to get their papers in on time, and that kind of thing. They conform pretty well. If the teacher asks a stupid question, a high IQ student may be able to give an intelligent answer, because he can sometimes translate the stupid question into the question that should have been asked and answer that one. This pleases the teacher.

"A student with high creativity but lower IQ doesn't show up so well. High creativity doesn't save him—as high IQ might—from giving a stupid answer to a stupid question. More typically, though, he may not do what the teacher wants because he is more interested in doing something else. Even though he might of his own volition be doing something pretty worthwhile, the teacher naturally thinks of him as being less dependable."

"It seems to me," said James, "that teachers *ought* to reward creativity. That's what I'd like to see."

"Oh, thank you," said John.

"Eh?" James was taken aback.

"But hard on you."

"What's hard on me?"

"So little reward. Or for IQ, either. Close correlation in your quartile, you know."

"Why, you big baboon. . . . " James sputtered, and Peter said to Professor Hilgard, "Please don't pay any attention to James and John, sir. *We* don't. They're brothers."

"Oh, I see," replied Professor Hilgard as if this explained everything. "Well, then, I should just like to finish by telling a little story.

"When I was in high school the administration decided to introduce a course in economics. They assigned it to the history teacher in the belief, I suppose, that she was a social scientist, economics was a social science course, and therefore she could teach economics. But it so happened that she had great difficulty in understanding economics. One of my best learning experiences in high school was getting together with other members of the class in order to explain economics clearly to our teacher, who was, in fact, quite ready to learn.

"For instance, we went to the bank for statements to prove to her that capital was listed as a liability and not as an asset, even though she knew capital to be an asset because her wealthy aunt occasionally had to dip into capital to pay her bills. In overcoming our teacher's objections, economics became clearer to everyone.

"I do not mean to say that this was good teaching. I only say that bad teaching sometimes has good results. After all, my economics teacher *was* interested and willing—and she liked us and we liked her. In such a good climate for learning, the best methods can't add very much nor the worst methods do much harm."

22
End of term

The lazy warmth of June came in the open windows, with a few notes of birds enjoying the shadows of late afternoon. It was the end of term. The seminar had come through the annual routine of reviewing our past meetings and summarizing for me (that I might know they had given some heed) what Professor Terman had said about steeples, Professor Polya about active learning, Professor Cowley about specialization, and Professor Kirkpatrick about research—even the twice-quoted line from Emerson had not gone unremarked. The seminar had done well, as indeed they always did, because their interest was genuine.

"Teaching and research are the jobs of faculty men," I said. "Are these the things that you look forward to doing?"

"I'm a research man," said Andrew. "I want to teach, too, but golly, it's a real thrill to find out something that's brand new, and then to write a paper to tell everybody about it."

"That's all right," said James, "but guiding young men to think in the right way seems to me a pretty fine thing, too."

"I doubt that I'll ever do very well at teaching," grieved Thomas. "There are such an awful lot of ways to go wrong."

"Of course you will," Peter encouraged him. "Besides, you've got to. Think how many good teachers are going to be needed. Why, they talk about the need for teachers being great now, but just think what it's going to be in a few years. It seems to me that the demand for teachers is just beginning and that it will grow and grow, because there's getting to be so much more to be taught. Why, if there's one thing sure . . . if there's one thing sure, . . . " Peter turned to me: "Do you mind, sir, if I prophesy a bit?"

"Go ahead," I said.

"It surely isn't going to be hard for you and me or any of us to find places to teach; colleges and schools are getting larger, and new ones are being opened every year. But part of that increase is because the population of the country is getting greater, and that isn't what I mean. Another part of the increase results from each student having to go to school longer now than he would have done ten years ago, and maybe that's what I'm talking about.

"There's more to know now than there was ten years ago or twenty years ago. There's more, that is, that a man has to know before he can be in the front rank with those who discover and design and develop new ideas. Let's say a guy named Jim Bright is in college today, and when he gets out he wants to be able to do the most advanced kind of work. He wants to be able to get a job at it, maybe doing research in a university or in a first-class industrial laboratory or in one of the better government labs.

"All right. He has to have a doctor's degree first. That means he will be getting on toward thirty years old before he gets out of school and starts looking for a permanent place. He could be as young as twenty-five if he went straight through and lost no time, but the chances are that he'll be at least twenty-seven or twenty-eight. I don't know how old all of you fellows are, but I expect you're about twenty-seven or -eight like me, and some of you are probably over thirty." Heads nodded.

"A few years ago there weren't so many doctor's degrees and fellows went to work much younger. Jobs were easier then, you'll say, and that's just my point. This guy Jim Bright will have to be nearly thirty before he gets into a good permanent place. Jim Bright's father on the other hand, might have stepped into a productive job in his early twenties, probably without a doctor's degree—they weren't so common then—but into a top quality, productive, creative job.

"Right now we hear a lot about postdoctoral fellowships, which I figure is a way of learning more about your particular speciality after you already have your doctor's degree. Suppose Jim Bright is going to have a postdoctoral for two or three years. By that time he'll surely be thirty or over.

"And so this thing goes on. Jim Bright and a thousand others like him will go into research labs in universities or industry or government and they'll discover more new things until Jim Bright's son goes to college, and it'll take him still more years to learn what he needs to know. It never gets less, it always gets more. The more research goes on, the more there is to know.

"How are we going to get Jim Bright's grandson through school before he's an old man? Well, one way is to limit him to a narrower specialty. This isn't the present trend—at least, everybody talks about a broader education, with more science and more mathematics and even more humanities, and nearly all these things do seem to be wanted by the best men. So—in the long run—scrub narrowness.

"Another way is to concentrate our subjects more, teaching more advanced material in earlier years. Well, we now teach to the freshmen what we used to teach to the graduate students, and I don't know how much farther this trend can possibly go. Already the business of shoving courses into earlier years has resulted in narrower education (which we say we don't want), and in making students work harder (or hoping they do), and in making everything more superficial, and of course in squeezing out all but the top-flight students (which may or may not be good).

"Or maybe we can do a better job of teaching. Maybe our teachers can waste less time. Maybe we can use psychology to teach better. Maybe the professors can be smarter.

"If none of these nice things can be done, or if they can only be done within limits—and that seems pretty certain—then Jim Bright, Jr. and Jim Bright III and IV are going to have to stay in school a long time before they can begin to contribute their bit to research or design; that is, to the use or advancement of knowledge.

"So what, you say. Maybe we lose a little time getting started, a few more years, but what of it? Just this: there's bound to be a limit. Every year that is needed for preparation is a year less for a man's productive work, and when you add to one you are subtracting from the other.

"But future generations of men will live longer, you say. Maybe they will; maybe they'll continue to live, but will they continue to produce? I once heard a professor ask a medical dean, 'Isn't it a fact that a man now has a greater life expectancy at age 65 than he used to have?'

" 'Yes,' the dean replied, 'but I don't know who would guarantee that he's going to be any smarter at the age of 65 than he used to be.'

"So nature sets an upper limit to productiveness. I don't mean to say that the upper limit is 65, either. You'll find plenty of psychologists to say that a physicist's most creative work is done before he's 35, an engineer's before he's 40, a mathematician's perhaps before he's 30. If these ages suggest the upper limit, we sure can't afford to keep raising the lower limit much higher than it is right now.

"All right. So what? We approach a limit—a limit beyond which human knowledge cannot progress. Will this limit be set by man's intellectual ability to do research? No, it will be set by the number of his productive years. And what limits the number of his productive years?—the speed and efficiency of his education. And what determines the speed and efficiency of his education?—the ability of his teachers.

"So what it comes to is this: the height to which mankind can aspire is set by man's ability to teach, to pass on the knowledge of one generation to the next. This ultimate level may not be reached for years and generations, but it will come—and when it does come we shall see the highest possible achievement of the human race determined by the wisdom of teachers."

* * *

"He told us that a book should end with a proper climax," said Peter.

"Golly, you've done it," said Andrew.

THE SEMINAR LEADERS:
who they are

William Harold Cowley   *Education*

AB, Dartmouth College; PhD, University of Chicago.

Teaching and administration: University of Chicago, Ohio State University, Hamilton College (president), University of Illinois, Stanford University.

Books: Occupational Orientation of College Students (with R. Hoppock, E. G. Williamson).

Gene Farthing Franklin   *Electrical Engineering*

BS, Georgia Institute of Technology; MS, Massachusetts Institute of Technology; DEngSci, Columbia University.

Teaching and administration: Columbia University, Cambridge University (England), Stanford University.

Books: Sampled-Data Control Systems (with J. R. Ragazzini).

Willis Walter Harman   *Engineering*

BS, University of Washington; MS, PhD, Stanford University.

Teaching and administration: University of Florida, Stanford University, Royal Technical Institute (Denmark); George Westinghouse Award (for teaching).

Books: Fundamentals of Electronic Motion; Principles of the Statistical Theory of Communication; Electrical and Mechanical Networks (with Dean W. Lytle).

Ernest Ropiequet Hilgard   *Psychology*

BS, University of Illinois; PhD, Yale University.

147

Teaching and administration: Yale University, Stanford University, member of U.S. Educational Mission to Japan.

Books: Conditioning and Learning (with D. G. Marquis); Theories of Learning; Introduction to Psychology; Hypnotic Susceptibility.

Paul Harmon Kirkpatrick   *Physics*

BS, Occidental College; PhD, University of California at Berkeley.

Teaching and administration: Hangchow College (China), University of Hawaii, University of California at Los Angeles, Cornell University, Stanford University, Bowdoin College, University of the Philippines, Dartmouth College, Wesleyan University. Awarded Oersted Medal by the Association of Physics Teachers.

Books: College Physics (with F. A. Saunders).

John Grimes Linvill   *Electrical Engineering*

AB, William Jewell College; SB, SM, ScD, Massachusetts Institute of Technology.

Teaching and administration: Massachusetts Institute of Technology, Stanford University, Technical Institute of Radio Engineering and Electronics (Prague, Czechoslovakia).

Books: Transistors and Active Circuits (with J. F. Gibbons); Models of Transistors and Diodes.

Malcolm Myers McWhorter   *Electrical Engineering*

BS, Oregon State College; MS, PhD, Stanford University.

Teaching and administration: Stanford University.

Books: Electronic Amplifier Circuits (with J. M. Pettit).

Joseph Mayo Pettit   *Engineering*

BS, University of California at Berkeley; EE, PhD, Stanford University.

Teaching and administration: University of California at Berkeley, Stanford University (dean of Engineering).

Books: Very-High Frequency Techniques (with others); Electronic Measurements (with F. E. Terman); Electronic Switching, Timing and Pulse Circuits; Electronic Amplifiers (with M. M. McWhorter).

George Polya   *Mathematics*

PhD, University of Budapest, Hungary.

Teaching and administration: Swiss Federal Institute of Technology (Zurich, Switzerland), Oxford and Cambridge Universities (England), Princeton University, Brown University, Smith College, Stanford University.

Books: Aufgaben und Lehrsätze aus der Analysis (with G. Szegö) (also in an American edition); How to Solve It; Isoperimetric Inequalities in Mathematical Physics (with G. Szegö); Inequalities (with G. H. Hardy and J. E. Littlewood); Mathematics and Plausible Reasoning; Mathematical Discovery: On Understanding, Learning and Teaching Problem Solving (two volumes).

Film: "Let Us Teach Guessing," a color film sponsored by the Mathematical Association of America.

William Craig Reynolds   *Mechanical Engineering*
BS, MS, PhD, Stanford University.
Teaching and administration: Stanford University.
Books: Thermodynamics.

Anthony Edward Siegman   *Electrical Engineering*
AB, Harvard University; MS, University of California at Los Angeles; PhD Stanford University.
Teaching and administration: Stanford University, Harvard University.
Books: Microwave Solid-State Masers; An Introduction to Lasers and Masers.

Hugh Hildreth Skilling   *Engineering*
AB, EE, PhD, Stanford University; SM, Massachusetts Institute of Technology.
Teaching and administration: Stanford University, Massachusetts Institute of Technology, Cambridge University (England). Awarded medal for education by the Institute of Electrical and Electronic Engineers.
Books: Transient Electric Currents; Fundamentals of Electric Waves; Exploring Electricity; Electric Transmission Lines; Electrical Engineering Circuits; Electromechanics.

Ralph Judson Smith   *Engineering*
BS, University of California at Berkeley; MS, EE, PhD, Stanford University.
Teaching and administration: San Jose State College, Stanford University, advisor on engineering education to Philippine Department of Education.
Books: Engineering as a Career; Circuits, Devices and Systems.

Frederick Emmons Terman   *Engineering*
AB, EE, Stanford University; ScD, Massachusetts Institute of Technology.

Teaching and administration: Stanford University (dean and provost), Harvard University (director of Radio Research Laboratory), Southern Methodist University Foundation of Science and Technology (president). Awarded medal (for teaching) by the American Institute of Electrical Engineers and the Lamme medal by the American Society for Engineering Education. In 1969 the American Society for Engineering Education established (with the support of the Hewlett-Packard Co.) the Frederick Emmons Terman prize for excellence in engineering teaching.

Books: Transmission-Line Theory (with W. S. Franklin); Radio Engineering; Measurements in Radio Engineering; Fundamentals of Radio; Radio and Vacuum Tube Theory (with U.S. Military Academy staff); Radio Engineers' Handbook; Electronic Measurements (with J. M. Pettit); Electronic and Radio Engineering.

David Fears Tuttle, Jr.   *Electrical Engineering*

AB, Amherst College; SB, SM, ScD, Massachusetts Institute of Technology.

Teaching and administration: Stanford University, École National Supérieure d'Électricité et de Méchanique (Nancy, France), Institut Polytechnique (Grenoble, France), École Superior de Physique (Marseilles, France), University of Madrid (Spain).

Books: Network Synthesis; Redes Electricas: Analysis y Sintesis; Electric Networks: Analysis and Synthesis.

John King Vennard   *Civil Engineering*

BS, MS, Massachusetts Institute of Technology.

Teaching and administration: Massachusetts Institute of Technology, New York University, Stanford University. Awarded Collingwood Prize by the American Society of Civil Engineers.

Books: Elementary Fluid Mechanics.